Orlando Ghosts

Rouse Road & Other Central Florida Haunts

Amanda Branham

Schiffer Publishing Ltd

4880 Lower Valley Road, Atglen, Pennsylvania 19310

Other Schiffer Books on Related Subjects:

Hauntings in Florida's Panhandle, 978-0-7643-3134-3, $14.99
Greetings from Daytona Beach, 978-0-7643-2806-0, $24.95

Schiffer Books are available at special discounts for bulk purchases for sales promotions or premiums. Special editions, including personalized covers, corporate imprints, and excerpts can be created in large quantities for special needs. For more information contact the publisher:

Schiffer Publishing Ltd.
4880 Lower Valley Road
Atglen, PA 19310
Phone: (610) 593-1777; Fax: (610) 593-2002
E-mail: Info@schifferbooks.com

For the largest selection of fine reference books on this and related subjects, please visit our web site at: **www.schifferbooks.com.** We are always looking for people to write books on new and related subjects. If you have an idea for a book please contact us at the above address.

This book may be purchased from the publisher. Include $5.00 for shipping. Please try your bookstore first. You may write for a free catalog.

In Europe, Schiffer books are distributed by
Bushwood Books
6 Marksbury Ave.
Kew Gardens
Surrey TW9 4JF England
Phone: 44 (0) 20 8392-8585; Fax: 44 (0) 20 8392-9876
E-mail: info@bushwoodbooks.co.uk
Website: www.bushwoodbooks.co.uk
Free postage in the U.K., Europe; air mail at cost.

Copyright © 2009 by Amanda Branham
Library of Congress Control Number: 2008939040

All rights reserved. No part of this work may be reproduced or used in any form or by any means—graphic, electronic, or mechanical, including photocopying or information storage and retrieval systems—without written permission from the publisher.
The scanning, uploading and distribution of this book or any part thereof via the Internet or via any other means without the permission of the publisher is illegal and punishable by law. Please purchase only authorized editions and do not participate in or encourage the electronic piracy of copyrighted materials.
"Schiffer," "Schiffer Publishing Ltd. & Design," and the "Design of pen and ink well" are registered trademarks of Schiffer Publishing Ltd.

Designed by Stephanie Daugherty
Type set in Parisian BT/NewsGoth BT

ISBN: 978-0-7643-3185-5
Printed in the United States of America

Contents

Acknowledgements

I would first and foremost like to thank both Emilio san Martin, the head of Haunted Orlando Ghost Tours, and Joseph, one of Emilio's tour guides and paranormal investigators, for their invaluable and generous help in navigating Orlando's haunted areas. Without their prior knowledge and assistance, this book would not have been possible.

Other thanks goes out to everyone: friends, family, and strangers on the street, all who encouraged this book and took interest. Thank you so much! I hope I can do you proud.

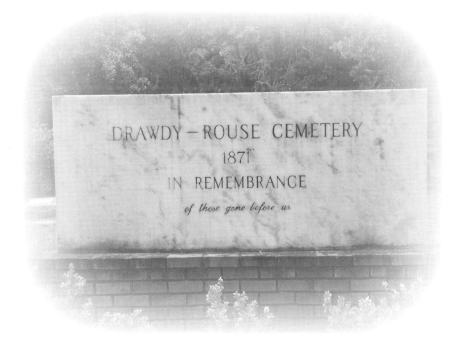

Introduction

I t's amazing how quickly people will talk to an almost complete stranger once the subject of ghost stories comes up. People who don't even know your name will start talking, telling you about their own experiences, tales their grandmothers told them, true stories that happened to a friend of a friend, and so on. Whether or not you believe in them doesn't matter; everyone has a ghost story to tell, and most people are more than happy to tell them. Almost everyone has that certain experience with an icy-cold touch on the back of their necks in a room they thought themselves alone in, or the sensation of being watched down a dusty hallway, or even a whispered voice in their bedrooms.

When I started this book, I thought I'd have the hardest time speaking one-on-one with people; I envisioned a lot of long, lonely hours spent in dusty corners of the libraries in the Central Florida archives, looking up possible ghostly sightings of the Oviedo Lights and Chuluota Road. Not so!

At the merest mention of haunted tales, people overhearing the conversation I was having with a friend or co-worker immediately started telling me their own experiences. Had I been to the Maguire House off of Highway 50? Had I mentioned Bloody Bucket Bridge? Did I know about so-and-so cemetery off of Rouse Road? Some I knew of, others I had no idea. A cornucopia of knowledge spilled out to me via word of mouth from people simply standing in line with me, or working an extra shift at work.

And I didn't even have to tell them I was writing a book.

I imagine a grubby looking lady with humidity-smeared make-up (me) was the last thing these crisp executive people wanted to see, especially one looking for a cemetery or a supposedly haunted bank. But as I literally went around from business to business, I found people who were more than happy to take a few minutes out of their day to sit down and speak with me. Suddenly, an austere manager was welcoming and the sweaty eccentric (still me) was interesting. Conversations started up, as good or better than the campfire tales I grew up hearing from Girl Scout troupe leaders.

Ghost stories do more than frighten us and send chills up our spines; they bring people together if for nothing more than the fact that everyone has heard one before. Chances are if you're reading this introduction, you've had an experience or two yourselves. Maybe you can't prove it's "real," but whether it's provable or not isn't the real point. The point is: it makes a great story. They can scare us, make us laugh, and make us check over our shoulders every once and a while.

More than half of the places I went to and researched, I didn't even know had a ghost story attached to it. I lived five minutes from Rouse Road for nearly five years without even knowing or guessing there was a cemetery near there, let alone that it was haunted. I grew up with the knowledge that Casadega, Florida was home to psychics and spirituals, and that St. Augustine didn't have an alleyway that *wasn't* haunted. But places like Oviedo, downtown Orlando, and Winter Park? Those places, home of boutiques and banks and farmland, had ghosts? I've learned that it's the seemingly "safe" corners that hold the scariest histories, the unpredictably haunted areas of an otherwise peaceful community.

The compilation of folk tales and ghostly sightings collected in this book was a huge joy to write, resulting in plenty of adventures and sleepless nights. I hope to have done justice to the haunted history of Orlando, Florida in bringing these tales to print. It often is surprising to learn that Central Florida has more to offer than tourism and Disney World; there's a few scares along the way as well. So without further ado, it's my pleasure to present *Orlando Ghosts, Rouse Road and Other Haunted Places of Central Florida*.

The Four Types of Hauntings

Otherwise known as, "So you've decided to be a paranormal enthusiast!", this section was written to help some readers, newer to the field of paranormal research, guide their way around both this book and any actual field work they may decide to do. A sort of Dos and Don'ts to the inside world, and what you may encounter during your own travels.

Before anything else is written, I must stress this: many places mentioned in this book were, in fact, private property with visiting hours posted. I urge anyone who may want to investigate both these places and others to abide by any rules posted. If the building is said to be haunted but it's condemned to be demolished and you don't have clearance to go in, take the rumors with a grain of salt and stay in your cars. Serious injuries or accidental death can occur if you're not careful; you don't want to end up being the *next* spirit haunting that place.

But first, what should you look for if you decide to do a bit of investigating of your own? While writing *Orlando Ghosts*, I discovered that speaking to people to get my first lead was the best areas to touch upon. From there, I dug up addresses and street names, contacted other, larger paranormal investigation agencies. "Haunted Orlando Tours," run by Emilio san Martin, was my best lead, and most helpful in pointing out where to go, and what the stories were behind several buildings. Without them, this book would never have happened. Asking for help from other, more experienced investigators can lead any would-be investigator in the right direction.

The best way to be prepared for any type of ghost hunting is to first know your area and what types of spirits you may be encountering. There are four basic types of haunts: *an intelligent haunt, object haunt, residual haunt, and poltergeist haunt*.

The First Law of Thermodynamics (also known as the law of conservation of energy) states that energy cannot be created or destroyed; it can only be changed. This brings up many interesting questions: if energy can't be destroyed, what happens to all of the energy in our bodies when we die? For those who believe we are more than working muscle and tissue, the soul or spirit of the body encompasses much of that energy. Some believe that should a person have a very strong personality, or have incredibly intense feelings before death, those feelings or that personality are stamped into the energy left behind, thus creating a haunting.

This theory is where many believe we get what is known as an *intelligent haunting*. An intelligent haunting is sometimes thought of to be the most "scariest" type of haunt because this is the type of haunting where the spirit will interact with you. This is where you get the poking, tugs on your shirt, spoken voices calling out for help, or whispering your name. Sometimes, they don't even know they're dead, and they want to be acknowledged. In some cases, if you speak to the spirit, acknowledge you know they're in the room, but would they kindly stop making the noise, they will stop for a few weeks. If the behavior of the spirit is more violent, it's a tricky situation if you want to give them acknowledgement. Depending on whom you ask, it's a yes/no situation; yes, give them acknowledgement that you know they are there and they don't frighten you, and no, don't acknowledge them because that gives them power over you.

If you do decide to interact with a spirit, asking questions can help, but whatever you do, do NOT ask questions such as "Are you going to kill me?" or "Are you going to follow me home and slaughter my family as we sleep?" Questions like this to *any* spirit, no matter how benign, will get you a lot of activity. Just imagine if you went up to a living person on the street and asked the same question. They'd give you just as many incredulous answers along the lines of "Good heavens, no, what is *wrong* with you?" You'll end up scaring yourself as one girl did during one of the Haunted Orlando Tours. Reality check: they will not follow you home and kill you and your family while you sleep, and on the off chance you do have an encounter with a violent spirit, you simply don't want to encourage any thoughts along that way. Just get out of the area as quickly as you can.

The second type of haunt is what is known as an **object haunting**. This is along the same lines as an intelligent haunt, except the spirit is attached to a particular object. These objects had a lot of sentimental and emotional value to the spirit while they were alive, and you'll likely see this with old wedding rings, jewelry of any kind, clocks, toys, and older antiques. Taking the object out of the house for a while is a good way of seeing if that object was causing the haunt or not.

If it is the object, but you really like that antique armoire in your bedroom and can withstand some bumps and creaks during the day, go ahead and keep it! But it's not advisable. Growing up in the days before electric stoves, my great-aunt had a wood-burning stove when she was a child. In an act of nostalgia (many) years later, she bought one just like it at an antique sale in Orlando and ended up with flickering lights and her dining room table and chairs constantly moved around the room. The next week, she brought it back to the people who sold it to her and told them to keep her money if they liked, but please, keep the stove somewhere else.

A quick search on eBay for "haunted objects" can bring an amazing array of supposedly haunted TV trays, rings, and even once, an old mayonnaise jar that the seller claims to have caught a ghost in. Whether or not it's true, be careful with what you buy with that intention.

A **residual haunt** is not attached to an object, but rather a particular place and chain of events that happened in that place. These spirits do not interact with anyone and they don't notice changes in their surroundings; they may look at you, but they do not see you. They're more apt to walk through walls or people or objects in their way because in their time, the table or wall or person was not there. It's debatable to know if they know they are gone from this life or not. I don't think they know they're dead. Most often, these hauntings play out much like a loop set on a movie, repeating over and over again. Battlefields – places where war broke out, where emotions were high and forceful – are the most common sites of residual hauntings.

Residual hauntings are actually where we get the idea of the white sheet "ghost" floating around, legless and transparent. One of the neatest stories I discovered on my local travels was that of an old dance hall in downtown Orlando. It's since been renovated into a themed 1950s hamburger joint (complete with a jukebox!), but in the early 1930s, it was a dance hall; when all is quiet, employees can sometimes hear the same faint song and see the same ghostly couples dancing through barstools and kitchen equipment, but from the shins down, there's nothing. This is because when the building was changed, the floor was elevated and changed; the original dance floor was kept about eight inches lower than the new floor is now.

The fourth, and last, type of haunting is what's known as a **poltergeist haunting**. Poltergeist, as many know, is German for "noisy ghost." Despite Hollywood hype and what a few popular television shows will have you believe, poltergeist activity is not synonymous with "demonic" activity. They aren't demons, and never have been. Many poltergeist activities revolve around young children and teenagers. Interesting, many types of poltergeist activity seems to revolve around teenage girls, leading many to believe the phenomena to be a latent ability for telekinesis without the child in question even knowing about it. Indeed, it seems the child and/or teenager will be the subject of such torment, hair pulling, things being smashed against walls, usually brought on by an upheaval in their security, such as puberty or perhaps a parent's divorce.

The only thing pop culture and the media seem to grasp about poltergeist that rings true are events shown where things are stacked or arranged in a different order than what they were originally were in. A scene in movies where a mother places the chairs against the breakfast table, turns around to put dishes away, and turns around again only to discover that the chairs are now stacked on top of one another half a minute later is an example of poltergeist activity. Poltergeists crave order; they need it. It's a little like having obsessive-compulsive disorder (OCD) of the paranormal world. It's an energy manifested from disorder, so the energy itself wants order for compensation. Think of it as your body suddenly craving a certain food when its potassium or vitamins are low.

The best way of proving whether a haunting is legitimate is to try and disprove it first. Going about a scientific method will give your findings more credibility; after all, there's a chance the scraping you here in the ceiling and walls is a spirit, but even more likely that it's rats, or a family of possums making their home in your attic. Be smart and be safe about it; never try and use an Ouija or spirit board to speak or communicate with anything, even in fun. One of the worst mistakes is to try and "make" your own ghost with one of these devices, especially in an area that's rumored to be rampant with paranormal activity. You just never know.

An interesting topic brought up for new and old paranormal investigators alike is how to get rid of a haunting. Can it be done? This question was brought up on a tour I took with Haunted Orlando, and the answer surprised me. It's an open ended mystery on how to get a ghost to leave; Hollywood loves to show the conclusion to an epic battle with ghosts versus humans, dire consequences, heavy gusts of wind from a spirit vortex, and a golden light before all is well. The truth is, it doesn't happen like that, and many of the spirits inhabiting the land of the living can never be forced to leave. Some of them will go dormant for a period of time, but that doesn't mean they've "crossed over" because someone made them. Spirits will go when they want to, and while there are some who believe an exorcism is the only sure-fire way of getting rid of a violent spirit, there are plenty of documented cases where a blessing or exorcism on a house didn't work for very long; I have personal experience with that.

Once a spirit realizes they're dead, they may move on, or they may want to stay for reasons known only to them. I think it's true they may stay on to help someone in need. The biggest thing for any interactive spirit is recognition; it's probably going to be the best bet in dealing with an unsavory situation with a ghost.

Always err on the side of caution with the paranormal; never go alone, and never go against your instincts. If the rational side of your mind tells you not to go into a certain building or piece of land...then listen to it. Essentially, we're all in tune to an unseen world; you wouldn't be interested in the idea of the paranormal if you weren't. Just always remember, the most important idea to keep in mind is to keep safe and open in your surroundings.

1

The Road from Daytona Beach into Orlando

D riving in Florida can be hazardous on its own without adding ghostly cars into the mixture of heavy traffic.

The path from Daytona Beach into Orlando is a lot of long stretches of roads with a lot of trees and wetlands in-between, and swamps and waterways perfect for air-boating. On late nights when traffic is down, when the road is desolate, the car without a driver can be seen.

No one knows where the story first surfaced; traffic accidents are dangerously common in Orlando, and so it's possible the phantom car has been shuffled away in case files long-forgotten, or marked as one too many late nights driving a long stretch of road that has the same monotonous background passing the drivers.

The car is often seen between just after sundown and midnight, driving erratically on the pavement, weaving throughout the lanes. Once seen, the car seems to know it's being watched and continues the dangerous antics until it careens off of the road, crashing into the underbrush off the highway.

Several calls have been made to the Florida Highway Patrol and many people have stopped off the side of the road where the car has crashed—only to discover there is *no* car at all. Just an empty roadside; no sounds of a crash, no tire marks, nothing. After several searches, it's probably labeled as a false alarm and people are left puzzling over what they know they've just seen. But it never makes any sense. The car – and whatever is driving it – is gone. Where it came from is unanswered, as to when it will show up again; sightings seem to be at random. Just a small "beware" warning for those coming to Orlando by way of Daytona.

Chuluota Road

✝✝✝✝✝✝✝✝✝

**Also known as State Road 419,
located right off of Highway 50**

✝✝✝✝✝✝✝✝✝

The long stretch of Florida road connecting East Orange County with Oviedo is not quite as desolate as it once was. Various subdivisions decorate what used to be a single lane road, a few churches, and a couple of stores before opening up to a wider gulf of busy intersections, but it's the main stay of the street people most want to avoid at night.

When I was a child, Chuluota Road was distinctly marked by a faded, orange-painted stucco wall with bold, green letters declaring CHULUOTA, and it remained so until the very late 1990s. Now it's a more subdued brown on tan, almost as if trying to not draw anymore unwanted attention. Nobody lingers on Chuluota Road after dark—not if they don't have to. It doesn't have the notoriety of the Dead Zone on Interstate 4, but to locals, it's the most common story you hear when you ask about haunted roads in Central Florida.

Every state has at least one haunted road that everybody knows about, talks about, and tries to avoid. It's spoken of amidst nervous laughter and every story told has the teller with wide eyes. What makes Chuluota eerie is less about something a person can see and more about something they can feel. If you walk around the edge of the dusty, wooded area by Chuluota Road, it feels like you're being watched. As many residents will tell anyone who bothers to ask, *"You just don't go into the woods at night."* It's more of an imprinted feeling you get in pockets; street lights rarely work down there, and when they do, they cast dim, orange lights that send shadows stretching to abnormally large lengths, adding to the overall creepy atmosphere.

Even in the most humid and balmiest nights, the woods around Chuluota will send shivers up and down your arms. It's the type of road no one wants to drive on alone; the type of road that, should you find yourself on, you look straight ahead and NEVER in your review mirror for fear of that one small chance you may find the reflection of a woman's face sitting in your back seat. So you stare entirely ahead until you see the convenience store lights and fast food chain restaurants ahead, welcoming you back into town.

Chuluota Road not only has a connection to the phenomena of the Oviedo Lights located off of Snow Hill Road, which are strange green balls of ghost lights that hover and sometimes chase those brave and foolhardy enough to go looking for them, but it's also home to some of the most foreboding woods around. One local man was willing to talk to me and he told me about his adolescent days—and how he never wanted to go out his back door at night.

"My job was to take out the trash; I always did it before sundown because the back of the house faced the wooded area, which was where we kept the trash cans before pick-up. Sometimes I'd peek out the screen door, but I always felt like something was watching me back, and I never stayed by the door for very long."

An imprint of an ominous feeling, one most citizens take very seriously, tells people very clearly to...'stay out'.

The sensation of being watched may be key to the phenomenon known as the Oviedo Lights. For years, teenagers have dared each other to drive down past what is now known as the intersection of Snow Hill and Chuluota roads, and just passed one of the many old bridges that pop up here and there on any Florida back road.

When the green glowing balls set their "sights" on you, they follow, sometimes chasing at a furious pace, other times in a more leisurely pace, and other times simply staying in one position. While some may claim these orbs are mere swamp gas, I've yet to hear a reasonable explanation for the chasing. Being lucky enough to spot one of these green orbs (or unlucky enough, depending on whom you ask) all comes down to location and time of evening.

The earliest stories I heard about the Oviedo Lights came from my aunt in the early 1980s, when Central Florida was still growing by leaps and bounds into the metropolis it is today. Teenagers would park their cars and start walking up and down Snow Hill Road, ducking into the dense, scrubby woods. When they'd gone in a few yards, far enough for any brave soul, eventually someone would call out the all-too familiar phrase when dealing with the paranormal:

"Did you hear that?"

Turning to look, someone would scan the horizon with a flashlight, eyes steady, hands shaking because who knew what could be out there? Maybe a few more steps would be taken, or maybe it was simply the act of someone turning around, but when the hovering green orbs would be seen, pandemonium would break out. Dropped flashlights and shouted profanities would fill the air as teenagers scrambled to get out of there. Sometimes the orbs would simply vanish, other times they enjoyed a chase, not stopping until the running kids got to their cars, out of breath and scared stiff, babbling incoherently amongst themselves.

"Did YOU see that?"

"No one is going to believe this."

"It touched me, I swear to God IT touched me."

Most accounts take place between well-after sunset and before 1 o'clock in the morning. What causes these lights to appear and hover, and sometimes even chase? Most skeptics chalk it up to be the humidity rising with pockets of swamp gas, but then how can the almost sentient behavior of follow and chase be explained? I'm not sure what the orbs are—spirits or energy imprints—but I am sure the amount of dropped flashlights in that score of woods and by the road could be counted in the hundreds, if not thousands.

The ghostly origins of the lights can be attributed to the story of a young man, who, after losing the woman he loved, committed suicide by jumping off of the bridge. A few people say they've seen the ghostly figure of a young man, even as the green orbs of light have been at their strongest, chasing any and all who dare enter his territory. It's also said that the orbs are more apt to chase lovers who come to find a semi-secluded place to hold hands and walk. It's a place well known to native Oviedo citizens, one that is either avoided or flocked to, depending on the mood to be scared or not.

It's easier to find Snow Hill Road now that Chuluota has been renovated and the roadways made larger, but it's no less ominous. A haunted road with a supermarket and quaint neighborhoods dotting the landscape *IS* still, after all, a haunted road.

Decendants of the founders of Rouse Road.

Rouse Road

His name was Benjamin Miles and by all accounts he is not a friendly spirit.

The medium-sized cemetery off of Rouse Road in the Orlando-Oviedo area would be almost pretty in an old, southern gothic way, save for the heavy, angry presence that cloaks the grounds. In the summer time, the dry grass almost seems to crackle with it; every step further and further into his territory leaves the visitor feeling more and more as though they ought to get out—and get out quickly. Even down the road, no one seems to feel safe until they're a good five miles or so away.

In 1840, Benjamin Miles, a Florida settler, died and was buried in an unmarked grave inside the cemetery. Could this be the reason for the haunting? Was Benjamin Miles so upset about being buried in an unmarked grave that he continues to walk the hallowed site? No one is certain, but his presence is filled with vehemence and anger.

In the middle of the night, usually around the fall and winter seasons, a sudden chill in the normally humid Florida air and the single call of an owl marks that Benjamin is near. Down the street at the bus stop, away from the actual cemetery, people have often remarked that they feel they're being watched, eyes are scrutinizing them. It gets especially bad if you find yourself there early in the morning, a stone's throw away from the cemetery grounds, before sunrise. You know when he's watching you; he's *always* watching. Miles, it's said, appears always in period clothing, usually tan or dark brown-looking work clothes, walking at a slow and steady pace toward the person he's been watching. Very few people will wait around to see what happens if he gets to you.

Mary-Lee Gladding shared her experience with me.

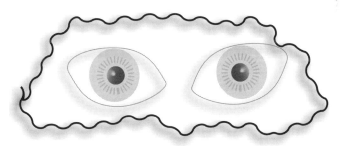

"I hate waiting at the bus stop early in the morning; it's so creepy out there. You just *FEEL* something watching you. It doesn't matter if you're alone or with someone...it's just as scary with another person near you."

✝✝✝✝✝✝✝✝✝✝✝✝✝✝

I went to Rouse Road to conduct my own mini investigation. It's private property and the hours are clearly posted: open from dawn until dusk. After my experience, I can't imagine going there at any time before the sun rises or after it sets.

I'm still not sure if it's the ghost stories or the landscape that makes it feel so unwelcoming. Though well kept and clean, there's a peculiar leaning to many of the older graves, some of which are propped upright only because there are trees growing directly behind them. Large, crooked trees, choked with thick coils of moss are everywhere—their jutting limbs and grey bark reminded me more of a gothic plantation from a turn of the century horror novella rather than a cemetery. But since the graveyard was founded in 1871, there's little surprise as to why it would feel as such.

I was intimidated to go inside. The day was hot and humid, and though the sun was hidden behind cloudy skies, it did very little to stave off the heat. There was no breeze, no wind to speak of, so everything was as still as the graves.

I was the only one in the cemetery that day; it's a fairly secluded road, only two lanes wide, with a smattering of houses tucked behind long driveways. I entered and closed the gate behind me, as there are several signs reminding visitors to do so, and set on my way. I wasn't sure where to start: legend says Benjamin Miles is buried in his unmarked grave towards the older section of the cemetery, in the back corner. It's hard to deduce which side of the medium-sized graveyard is the "older" section, as many of the graves are dated from the 1800s.

I didn't want to start out jumping headlong into the fray; I admit it, I was scared to be there. It's a pressing place, feeling every bit as forboding and heavy as the stories I had heard second-hand from other people, and I had broken my very first rule about venturing into active places by going alone. I suppose I did it because I had doubted many of the stories I heard, halfway in my mind wondering if they were really true. Despite my own encounters with the paranormal before, I remained a doubting Thomas until I had proof I could see and hear first-hand. Skeptical is my middle name. I circled around the first grouping of graves.

Startling, there are so many graves of young children at the front, many living and dying the same day, from the late 1800s to early 1900s. Most of the inscriptions, chosen by grieving parents, proclaim everlasting love, that the children left them to become angels, small sayings from the *Bible* in order to give them hope. It's little wonder the cemetery seems to have a feeling of loss and anger.

I took many pictures, close-ups of the graves. Many of them are so old and not taken care of; the inscriptions have been washed away by age and environment, leaving rounded corners and dark surfaces. A few of the headstones have a variety of angels kneeling by them, as equally aged as the stones. One in particular stood out, placed next to a rounded stone of a young girl who died surely before her time. The angel was dark with muck and headless, kneeling in prayer by its deceased. There are plots with benches installed right next to the graves; I was surprised

Many of the headstones are like this, almost impossible to tell what the graves say.

A headless angel statuette. Macabre and creepy, much like Rouse Road Cemetery itself is.

by the urge I had to take pictures of a few plots in particular. It felt as though there was someone there, sitting on the bench visiting the graves...*maybe there were*. While snapping pictures, I didn't capture any orbs that showed up on my computer when I transferred the pictures from the memory card to my laptop, however there were colored lines I saw through the viewing screen before I pressed the shutter, as well as a smoke-like substance rising from the leaves and trees.

A camera error? Or something that truly didn't want to have its likeness caught on film? I don't know, and that was slightly more nerve-wracking than I would have cared to admit. While alone in a graveyard, the last thing you want to be wondering is, '*What the heck is that*?'

As I made my way to the middle of the cemetery, dodging the sprinkler system, I noticed a scattering of graves that were all older and snapped more pictures. The thought occurred to me that perhaps if I tried, I could get some EVPs.

Interesting symbols on a headstone. A few people have thought they might be Shriner symbols.

A rather disquieting statuette at Rouse Road.

EVP stands for **Electronic Voice Phenomenon**, a standard way of grabbing proof of a haunting, made popular by more recent movies and television shows promoting the paranormal. I thought it would be as easy as it looks on television, like on "Ghosthunters," where TAPS investigators pull out their recorders and go to town. Clearly, there's more to it than what is shown on television, and I now have a better understanding for what those investigators go through. *(TAPS stands for The Atlantic Paranormal Society, a group that investigates supposed haunting phenomenon all over the United States.)*

My method was slightly less in depth and professional; I only had my cellular phone with a voice-recording feature installed in the electronic organizer. It's interesting how self-conscious a person can feel when speaking into the air to no one living, holding a cell phone around, asking if anyone had anything to say. I would not have been surprised if a spirit voice had recorded itself saying, 'Yes, you're annoying and crazy. Go away.'

The first five recordings I took, I could only hear a muffled static sound, sounds I weren't sure if they were proof of activity or proof the sprinkler system was still on behind me.

There was one EVP I took, and even now it leads me to believe that Benjamin Miles is not the only spirit possibly haunting the Rouse Road Cemetery. I hadn't bothered asking any of the usual questions with this EVP attempt (Is anyone there? Do you have anything to say? Can you tell me your name? Are you happy here?—I'm still not sure what I was thinking when I asked if they were happy there. They're dead and in a haunted cemetery. How happy could they be?). I simply held the record button and held it out in front of me. At this point, I had worked up the nerve to make my way to the back of the property. I held it there for about half a minute before pressing stop. I hadn't heard anything while recording, but later, back in my car, there was a faint screaming sound, female in tone and pitch.

Another oddity in the cemetery were two headstones marked "LOFTIS." The headstone to the right had an upside down pentacle professionally carved into the stone, where as the one on the left had a symbol I was not familiar with. But in a plot filled with baby angels and shepherds, seeing something out of the norm like this was interesting. The other interesting point I noticed was the amount of dead insects scattered across the ground of these two headstones; the rest of the grounds were well kept, so why were these the only ones with dead beetles and bees scattered around?

But I had come there for proof of ghosts, and one in particular. The only EVP I got was a response to a question I asked shortly before I left. I left as quickly as I did as a result of the response I got. Standing with my cell phone set on record, I asked aloud: "Benjamin Miles! Benjamin Miles,

Around the back of Rouse Road Cemetery...where I heard the voice telling me to "Go."

are you here?" Recorded into my phone was an answer even I could hear with my weak human ears: a groaning sound that clearly said, "Go." It was a drawn out moan, soft and ultimately unhappy.

"Gooooo...."

It was time to GO. There are times when someone is struck by fear and surprise and can't move for a few minutes. I've had that happen to me once before in my life, and the feeling is very distinct. When I heard the faint moaning again, closer this time, there was a prickling sensation on my face, and I made my legs start moving, as I looked for the quickest way out. My heart was a few steps ahead of the rest of my body, beating quickly as though it wanted to jump out of my chest. My doubt that there wasn't anything in the cemetery was long gone.

I didn't get the sense that it was Benjamin Miles, the famed spirit. Even as I heard it, the thought that popped into my head was, "This is a warning, and I need to go." Much like reciting the name of a boogey-man or Bloody Mary, I believe it was the very mention of the name that prompted another spirit to call out their short warning—I had crossed the line and needed to go.

I walked quickly to the front of the property, and stopped short again. The gate I had closed and latched behind me was open, drag marks in the soft dirt where it had been set, as though ushering me on my way. My face was still prickling, stinging a little where I was sweating, but I wasn't about to stop, pull out a compact mirror and check. I looked around to see if there was perhaps another visitor had come in behind me that I had not yet noticed. But, no...I was still alone.

Taking this as an ultimate sign I was no longer welcomed and needed to leave, I did so, latching the gate behind me again. It wasn't until I was back in my car and starting the engine that I noticed two thin, curved scratches on my face; one on my forehead

A picture of the gate as I jogged my way out of the cemetery... it had unlatched itself and opened up, despite my being the only person inside.

above my eyebrow and the other on the bridge of my nose. They weren't horribly long, but they were red.

When I spoke to my co-worker, Mary-Lee, about the incident, she nodded her head. "You were probably starting to get him angry. You're lucky you got away with just some scratches on your face."

"What do you mean?" I asked. I wasn't confused, but rather curious. I didn't doubt the stories I had heard now about angry spirits, but I was anxious to know what other stories Mary-Lee might have. She'd been on a few ghost hunts herself with friends of hers and knew more about it than I did.

"Two friends of mine trespassed after dark back in October at the Rouse Road Cemetery. I didn't go in, but I could hear what was going on."

Apparently, the foolhardy friends didn't get a chance to stay too long.

"They came running back out, saying they'd had chunks of the ground fly up at them. Stupid idiots, I told them not to go in there!" Scared stiff, Mary's friends vowed never to go in there again, day or night. Mary-Lee, for her part, won't go in there at all.

"Not a chance," she said when I extended an invitation to go back there. However, when I mentioned the possibility of the voice I heard *not* being Benjamin Miles, she agreed with me. "If it were Benjamin Miles, you'd have gotten more than just a couple of scratches," she said.

Is it possible there might be *another* restless spirit at Rouse Road, perhaps to warn other people?

"Probably, it was telling you to get out, especially if you were stirring Benjamin Miles up," Mary-Lee said. "There's just too much going on in there. It's why I don't set foot in the place."

Reviewing the film I had taken at Rouse Road Cemetery, I was both surprised and not surprised to find several pictures blank from my memory card. Some forces do not want to be proven, and if I ever doubted what the Rouse Road Cemetery had before, I certainly don't now. After all, the sign in front of the cemetery even says "In remembrance of those gone before us."

2

Haunted Schools

Oviedo High School

S chools in Orlando, Florida seem to have a running streak of haunted activity. Oviedo High School is one of several such schools in the Orlando area with reported haunted activity surrounding its auditorium, and this auditorium is home to more than just plays and talent shows.

Theatre ghosts have always been a main staple in folklore... dramatic souls tend to be pulled towards the stage, rather than off of it. It is their domain in life, so why not in the afterlife? And high schools, with their students growing and changing often at a dramatic and frenetic pace, have a high energy around them to begin with. So why should a high school auditorium be any different?

The theatre at this particular school doesn't seem to have a predominantly vindictive haunting, unlike the rest of the campus. Many tales of Oviedo High School's auditorium and stage feature strange and unexplained flashing lights, accompanied by the faceless figure. While no features are present on this figure, no one has claimed to feel threatened by an overwhelming presence. Though the flashing lights are considered to be a bit unusual and disconcerting, there have been no murmured warnings, no decimated stage sets. But no one can deny that suddenly looking over a shoulder to find a faceless figure with flashing lights is more than a little creepy.

Most staff and students of the high school agree the figure is harmless; "he's" less likely to prank a person and more likely to simply make his presence known.

The same cannot be said for the *other* spirit more commonly seen on campus.

Reports and rumors of another, though nameless, ghost seen have occurred not just in the girls' dressing room at the auditorium, but at other locations on the school grounds as well—and the activity has not been nearly so benign. She has a sad face, pale and listless as if she's been recently crying. With her long, limp brown hair, the female ghost of Oviedo High School seems to want to be noticed. Her dress has even appeared as blood-spattered.

Reports of the female ghost stalking and following students for a few days is not unheard of; as the stories go, she latches on to more sympathetic people and will follow them around school, and even, as a few tentative students have claimed, to their homes off campus. She will try to tell you her story, even try to scare the people she follows, as if frustrated that no one can understand her. If you're in a classroom by yourself, after everyone else has gone, it's the perfect time for you to hear her.

It takes days for her to move on, picking through the people she reveals herself to as though searching for someone, or maybe, no one in mind at all. But once she latches onto you, there seems to be no escape until she, *and ONLY she*, decides to go on to the next person. There is no part of the legend that gives much explanation to say whom she was or when she went to school there, if she did at all.

Evans High School

Evans High School reportedly has its share of hauntings as well. This ghost is said to haunt their auditorium also, but his activity stays solely on the catwalk above the stage. Believed to be the spirit of a man who hung himself in the school gym in the 1960s, this high school ghost doesn't trail students around.

Scraping noises above the stage can be heard, as though someone is moving around when no one is up on the catwalk or even on the stage itself. Lights have been reported to go on and off without anyone (anyone living, that is) working the controls. The overall consensus of the ghost is that he simply wanders around the school; he doesn't want to scare anyone, he just simply doesn't want to move on.

Since his activity has been limited to turning on lights and walking around above a stage, it seems accurate that this is one theatre ghost not bent on causing mischief; no howling, no locked doors, no following students or faculty. It's slightly melancholy to think about, and perhaps one of the few spirits to invoke pity rather than fear.

Documented cases of puberty bringing on an onset of haunted activities are not rare; many people believe that the strong emotions and unstable hormones of teenagers will often invoke a sort of beacon to the spirit world, beckoning them.

University High School

University High School has its own tale of a catwalk ghost as well. This spirit seems to be a former janitor who was said to have fallen to his untimely death while up on the high beams in the auditorium. Former and current students have stated they can see an outline of a male figure, walking and checking the lights, and they claim that the scent of cigarette smoke will sometimes accompany the figure.

As an alumnus of University High School, and a Thespian of Troupe 4848, I spent many hours in the school's auditorium and on stage. I never went up to the catwalk to see if I could find a spirit myself, so I cannot claim first-hand knowledge. But I can say I was too frightened of my friends' serious tones and frank manner when they told the tales of our school's resident ghost to doubt them enough to see for myself. I was always told he was a harmless spirit, proceeded by a jangling clink of keys and loose change on the catwalk; perhaps the most disturbing thing was that he would stop and suddenly run right at you, urgently, as though he had something to tell you. I was never sure if I could handle that. Even so, there were no horrible smells, moaning sounds, or dire warnings of death with University's unconfirmed spirit hanging around. By far harmless and simply "there," I wonder if anyone since I've graduated has tried to go up to the catwalk and see the ghost for themselves.

Union Park Elementary School

When visiting Orlando, whether it's to go around Disney World or many of the other theme parks, or visit a potential new home, surprises await around every corner. At Union Park Elementary School, a young maiden named Mary haunts the girl's bathroom on the lower level. It's unclear how long Mary has been at the school; it's said she always appears in a long white dress.

Mary is rumored to be the daughter of a former janitor at the school, but no one can say for sure if she was a student there, or how she died. Based on the sightings, most guess Mary's age between seven and nine, so it's not unreal to imagine Mary was a student at Union Park Elementary School.

When Mary is around, the bathroom seems to be her favorite place to gravitate to; she is not often seen as a physical manifestation, but rather prefers to stay invisible to the human eye. Sinks begin to shake and doors open and close by themselves; while shy to appear before people, Mary is more mischievous and playful than vindictive or scary. Loud thumping sounds can be heard, echoing in the nearby stalls, and sometimes a faint yell or cry can be heard in the hallways by the bathroom. It doesn't sound like a cry of fear, more like the rambunctious yell of a young girl playing in school.

As to whom Mary's mother or father was, no record can be found of her custodial parent, or how long he or she worked there, but no one at the school tends to be disturbed by Mary's presence. Instead, she seems to be counted in a special group of students who just never seem to leave.

3

Haunted Bridges

Bloody Bucket Bridge

I t's difficult to pinpoint the exact origin of Bloody Bucket Bridge; the legend itself was told to me by my friend Janelle, and confirmed by my co-workers. Oviedo, much like the rest of Central Florida, is an interesting mix of rural and urban. Go five miles down—yes, you guessed it—Chuluota Road or Aloma Avenue and you've gone from the mall to cow fields and the interstate merges into pockets of country lanes.

It's here in the seemingly time-forgotten place, deeper in Oviedo, that rumor of the past whispers a more macabre history. Long used to friendly jabs at free-range chicken herds that roam free in the streets, it's no surprise that the folklore of Bloody Bucket Bridge is kept quiet, far more so than the Oviedo Lights.

There are a few variations to the tale. As I originally heard it, in the late 1880s, in a more remote portion of the "city," a certain mid-wife was relied heavily upon for most of the births delivered. When a woman's birth pains began, this mid-wife was called for immediately. She would arrive and begin her work.

Long, arduous deliveries happened more often than not, and even experienced mothers tended to have difficult pregnancies and births. Throughout the night, the mid-wife would be seen walking back and forth from the house to the small bridge near town to drop the bloodied rags into the river. She'd use an old bucket with a rope tied to the handle in order to scoop the water up to cleanse the rags of the various fluids brought on by her trade.

In a time of economic decline, birthrates rose and kept rising, despite the families dwindling supply of food, clothing, and space. Speculation says the mid-wife saw the decay and hard living around her and made a slow descent into madness.

If, she decided, the people wouldn't stop having children they couldn't care for, she would help them in another way.

After that, once the mid-wife was called, infants in her care mysteriously began dying. The tale goes that once the child was placed into its crib, she'd smother the poor baby and carry its lifeless body into the parents, feigning shock and dismay. Other tales say she'd deliver the baby, smother its cries, and immediately declare the child to be so malformed and misshapen as to not be fit to be seen by either parent. Back and forth she walked to the bridge, taking her bucket filled with the after-birth and bloodied rags, dumping the remains into the river to be washed away. In yet another, more gruesome telling, the mid-wife took the remains of the infant, dismembered them, and tossed those into the river along with the rags and blood somehow without anyone knowing it.

It didn't take very long to discover that the infants died once in her care, and in a mob-like formation, the mid-wife was arrested and hung. She cried out that she was doing it only for the children's own good; better the child die before it knew what pain was, than to starve and feel the wrath of disease. The overpopulation would mean death to them all, she claimed.

But her pleas and reasoning did nothing to persuade the enraged crowd, several of whom claim to have heard their poor murdered babies crying in the late hours of night. In all of the accounts, the mid-wife met her end by being hung, not half a mile from what people were now calling Bloody Bucket Bridge.

An alternate account of this tale says an influx of unmarried mothers giving birth caused the mid-wife to not only kill those infants, but also the young mothers-to-be. In this version, the mid-wife carried on for years, secretly killing the babies born out of wedlock and their unfortunate mothers who birthed them, claiming the ravages of a rough labor was simply too much for these women and babies to bear.

Rumor is, you can only find the spot where the dinky bridge used to host the walking in the dilapidated woods in Oviedo. It's small and unsteady over the stream of mostly stagnant water, home to amateur ghost hunters and groups just looking for a good scare, trying to spot the telltale sign or howl of the monstrous midwife. They say you'll know when you find it between the hours of 9 p.m. and 3 a.m. by hearing the thumping of the midwife's footsteps on the ground of a wooden bridge and the accompanying cries of the infants surrounding her, following her for the rest of her afterlife. It's possible to even catch a glimpse of a hooded woman, dumping the silhouette of a bucket over a bridge that has long been unused by any living persons, or so I have been told.

Little Econ River

When my Aunt Marlene first told me the story behind Little Econ River, she began like this: "I can't swear if all the spirit talk is true, but I remember Christopher Klink, so I wouldn't doubt it." 'Killer Klink,' as he was called, seems to be haunting the bridge by the Econlockhatchee River, and appears to be the only ghost in Central Florida with a specific date for his haunting.

Every October 13th, the spirit of the killer, Christopher Klink, will appear. There is no sound of footsteps, but rather something more sinister and otherworldly. There is a chill in the air, biting at any exposed skin, followed shortly after by the flow of the river's water stopping and going in reverse. Reflective light will hover and somehow manage to fall on Killer Klink's tag, written under the bridge. His 'tag' is a date, written by Klink himself: October 13 1987.

The spirit of Killer Klink is then seen hanging from the bridge. As my aunt told it, Klink had murdered several women and thought himself free of any charges, until this very date of October 13th when members of the families of the women he killed found and caught Klink and beat him to death right under the very bridge.

The spirit doesn't interact with anyone; only the solitary body, hanging and swinging to and fro from a bridge. It seems he is doomed to repeat this year after year. Eternal punishment after a very mortal, non-judicial "court" decided his fate and administered the sentence? Or perhaps something more permanent to mark the place where a killer hung, more permanent than a carved tag? Only after the apparition of his body disappears do the frigid cold air warm to normal temperatures and the water returns to its regular flow.

4

Haunted Streets

Andrew Street, Anders Street, & Chapman Road

The image of children in pigtails or overalls playing isn't uncommon in Florida, despite the heat, especially in Orlando. The flat fields, even if bare of playground equipment, can still be an imaginative play area in the minds of innocent children. Even deceased ones.

Andrew Street isn't an overly long, well-traveled road; it's easy to miss in this sleepier part of Oveido where the more rural land juts out, imposing on the malls and highways. Tucked away, these nearly hidden roads pass by equally fallow grasslands. Tales of children playing in the fields of Andrews Street aren't unheard of; the witnesses often don't even know they're ghosts until they all simply disappear into nothingness, so quickly, the people doubt what they've just seen. In the span of a blink, they don't fade from sight, but rather, are simply gone as though they were never there. The feeling around these fields tends to be happy and playful most of the time, but a few people have heard a small, lisped whisper of "Help me" once or twice. The spirit of the plaintive request never shows him or herself, and so an answer is never given as to who or what needs help.

But, despite these conflicting encounters, most can agree on the sightings of children running around in the field. It isn't surprising to hear, considering miles down, away from Andrew Street, a place called Anders Street is also haunted by the presence of running and playing children. The two roads don't connect and are a considerable distance away from each other, so it's strange that they would both have a similar haunting.

What's left of the old celery field is not open to the public; in fact, it's a bit off the beaten path, developed into sub-divisions and neighborhoods. In the time that neighborhoods cropped up around, and even, in the once-vast celery fields, the crops may have been cleared away but the spirits of children playing remained. Now, sightings of ghost children wandering around the neighborhood are common. They look confused, even sad; they're not sure where they are, or what happened to their play field.

Well-meaning parents will go up to one such lost looking spirit, asking if he or she is lost and if they know where they live. The child may look up at them...and then disappear without a trace. Sightings of the children who play alone in the celery fields are not new either; dividing the land up and carving the borders have done nothing to discourage spirits from finding ways to make themselves known, even adult ones.

Down a dirt road, not far from Anders Street is another field, this one intact, where living parents do not let their children go alone, if at all. This field, thought to be a part of the same old celery plot, is smaller, but no less active with snippets of ghosts. The figure of a man in a suit carrying a briefcase has been seen walking towards and in between the two pillars that stand there by the electrical fence. There he stands, never moving, never speaking; it seems he does not hear or see anything but his destination. Even still, despite the man, children's laughter is often heard, sometimes the children are even seen, playing games long into the night; but despite this sinister description, no one has come forward to say this old field has felt anything like Rouse Road Cemetery. The atmosphere has been peaceful, almost playful, with no added whispering voices calling for help.

Further still on Chapman Road, which Anders Street abuts, the pavement turns to gravel and grit, more dirt and shell than road. This is where the fields open up more and where two telephone poles sit. No development has occurred in a number of years. Not a particularly chilling sight, or an uncommon sight in Florida, but what is uncommon is the amount of mists that sit between these two poles at night—no matter what the weather is. Drivers going down this road are boggled by the sight, the mists settling between these two poles and nowhere else, but what turns the mists from merely an odd sight to something a little creepier are the screams that people hear as they drive down the road. Sometimes, it's not even after the sun goes down; in the middle of the day, twilight, or midnight, you can hear the screams echoing around. They're short, punctuated kind of screams, as though an unseen force is cutting it off. At first, it's easy to dismiss the screaming sounds as over rambunctious neighbors until a look around confirms there are no houses close by these particular electric poles; only a dirt road and a dead end—no pun intended.

5

The Dead Zone

As with any populated city, Central Florida has its share of traffic accidents along its interstates and highways. But how many other states in America can claim ghostly activity for the reason of the gridlock and traffic accidents? Or even a hurricane's unnatural maneuvering across a state and an ocean?

I first heard of the Dead Zone by word of mouth from my friend Janelle. She's also somewhat of a paranormal buff, devouring strange accounts like a starving person. She can rattle off statistics, dates, and strange occurrences faster than an Internet search engine. I'll cross check references by her before I'll even consult "Google."

There are four graves under an overpass, just north of Orlando. It's only a quarter mile long, but it's one of the most deadly areas of highway Florida has to offer. The official name of this stretch of highway is Interstate 4, more commonly reduced to the nickname of I-4, but many more people refer to it as the Dead Zone. To date, the local news channels have reported some 2,000 plus deaths happening on this overpass, dating back from 1963, when the highway was fully constructed.

It started during the Yellow Fever epidemic of 1887. There was little hope for the small Roman Catholic colony known as St. Joseph's Colony, when the fever struck. They had little provisions, no doctors, and just when things did not seem like it could get any worse, the colony's priest died, leaving the congregation

Early times at the colony before the fever outbreak.
Courtesy of Mike Holfeld and the Orlando Museum.

without leadership or prayer and no way to bless the graves. The epidemic continued, uncaring that those who died now would not be blessed in their graves. A family of four soon succumbed to the disease that rampaged around the colony, and the rest of the citizens had little choice but to simply bury the poor unfortunates without a proper ceremony in four plain, but marked, graves.

It has been noted that the graves were very clearly marked and placed, and when Albert Hawkins bought the land for farming in 1905, he found the four graves and kept a respectful area cleared for the miniature cemetery. Though it sat in the middle of his farmland like a rather macabre island onto itself, there were no problems to be had. Hawkins seemed to have a mutual understanding with the graves and kept the field tidy; he did not flinch in his self-brought on responsibility, even as the farm became known as the Field of the Dead to the other locals. While he tended the graves, the fact that there were four (unblessed and unsprayed over) graves on his land was not something Hawkins nor his wife advertised to the world; it became a rather well kept, yet open, secret that no one in the population near the still-rural land seemed to want to share with the outside world.

Even after Albert Hawkins died in 1935, his widowed wife stayed and kept the land. It was not until 1960, when Orlando started becoming more of a suburban area, developing more roads, more employment opportunities, and more houses, that

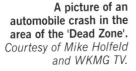

A picture of an automobile crash in the area of the 'Dead Zone'.
Courtesy of Mike Holfeld and WKMG TV.

the land was bought from the Hawkins family to be used in the new Interstate 4 Highway. State surveyors were alerted to the location of the meager resting place in the old farmland, but for whatever reason, the graves were not moved and reburied in a churchyard. In a decision reminiscent of a horror film, the graves were simply trampled on and hundreds of pounds of dirt were dumped upon the graves in order to elevate and level the land in preparation for the new highway.

What followed next seemed almost like an Aesop tale, complete with the moral to the story. No sooner had the dirt been dumped and leveled out than Hurricane Donna, one of the worst hurricane storms to hit Central Florida in a century, crossed over the state. The eye of the storm went and stayed directly on the area the graves had been, eerily making a zigzag pattern well into the initial break on land, as though sentient thought called the storm to unleash its fury and flood over the new construction site. What shook many people was the path of the storm; it seemed drawn to the graves after crossing over from the Atlantic Ocean and making land fall in South Florida and crossing the state completely. But while the storm was in the Gulf of Mexico, it suddenly turned, heading up the portions of Interstate 4 already completed. The eye of Hurricane Donna was seen hovering over the graves around midnight after its second land break before exiting by way of Ormond Beach.

The damage done by the storm was so great, it canceled any plans to move forward with the interstate's construction for several months. The complicated maneuver of the storm, its second hit on the land, and the sheer flooding it caused made many people suspect it was the work of the dead, payback for tampering with their final resting place.

This did little to stop progress though, and eventually the overpass was finished and connected. But the ghosts have not left. Several drivers report picking up their cellular phones, only to hear strange voices talking and overlapping each other, while others claim the voices will interrupt conversations if the phone is still in use. Sightings of ghostly hitchhikers are often seen, four in total, and it's not uncommon to hear that more accidents happen on that stretch of highway than anywhere else. Many drivers will explain that they swerved to avoid hitting what looked like a family of four simply walking across the overpass; some drivers are even convinced they've hit one or two of the people. But there's never anyone found—no bodies and no sign that anyone had been there at all.

Radios are not off limits to this tampering either; often people will hear a perfectly clear signal turn diluted and static-filled, and some even claim to hear voices whispering through their car speakers. Strange, white floating mists and balls of light zipping from one side of the highway to the other are seen in the evening, closer to the midnight hour, making me wonder if midnight was the hour when the family members died. The unusually high number of traffic accidents has even caught the eye of local news stations, and most Octobers find the "Dead Zone" getting a lot of coverage due to that Halloween feeling in the air.

Despite the cynicism often associated with the world of the paranormal, despite that the words "deadly stretch of I-4" usually have quotations around the word "deadly," giving it a somewhat sarcastic tone, I know several people who simply refuse to drive on I-4 because of the Dead Zone. The proof is in the sights of crumpled cars, foggy mists on photographs, and hundreds of spooked drivers.

This stretch of road is perhaps the only place I did not go to in person, because I didn't feel it was safe. Not only for the ghost stories surrounding the area, but also the knowledge of the graves being under the road. I will neither drive on this interstate, nor visit there, and I urge anyone who feels the need to visit the Dead Zone in person to do so with extreme caution. It's not a country road you can stop on the side of and take pictures at your leisure—it's a busy and dangerous stretch of road.

As for my own experience with the Dead Zone, I can honestly say I have never had one. I don't drive on I-4 when travel demands I take a highway, and I don't recommend anyone going to Lake Monroe's bridge to find that quarter mile of road at high speeds and heavy traffic. It's a Florida legend I first read about in a book by Charlie Carlson, *Weird Florida*, and had seen on my local news stations. The story struck something in me and my curiosity of seeing "if it was true" was satisfied by what had been reported on the subject by others before me. I don't know why this one place, out of all the others I've been to, felt "off limits" to me, but I took it for a reason and did not go.

6

Haunted Cemeteries and Fields

St. Luke's Cathedral & Cemetery

T he church and subsequent cemetery known as St. Luke's Cathedral was started and enlarged in 1892, out in Oviedo. The cathedral itself, both impressive and beautiful, started out with a meager flock of devoted parishioners that eventually grew to fill an entire monument. With its stained glass windows and high archway, not only does St. Luke's have its own cemetery, but it also houses a private school.

In Orlando's earliest beginnings, many communities were still faintly nomadic; there were very few burial plots that were formally recognized as graveyards. Oftentimes, families simply buried their loved ones in the yards, or out in their fields. This being the case, it's heavily speculated that St. Luke's Cathedral's construction may have actually disturbed quite a few resting places itself.

But even if that is true, the majority of this beautiful, yet haunted, location focuses mainly on the cemetery across the street. In the small building near the very end of the cemetery, there in the corner, a very threatening presence is felt. Oddly enough, it's as far from the actual church as anything can get and still be on the property. Oftentimes, visitors entering the cemetery will feel their breath constricting, and if they venture further into the fenced off cemetery, it just gets harder and harder to inhale.

More often than not, the further in someone goes, his or her hands begin to tingle as well, almost like a warning sign. Upon leaving the gated cemetery, people have complained of welts and red marks raised on the flesh of their necks and shoulders, as though something tried to grab and claw at them, but none can remember feeling it at the time they were in the cemetery.

No sounds, no EVPs have ever been picked up; it is a silent place with only the sound of a passing car to break that silence. Even stranger, since this is still a fairly rural area, little to no sounds of animals of insects are ever heard or seen near this location. Is there truly a presence driving all living things away from this resting place? Something moved before the cathedral's time of creation? I could not imagine what or who it would be, only that it stays well away from the actual sanctuary of the church.

Oviedo Baseball Fields

A lot of expectations surround America's favorite pastime. There are certain events people expect to see: spectacular catches, near misses, sliding into home base. But ghosts?

Apparently so, on Oviedo's Baseball Field, used mostly for youth baseball games. Sightings of a Native American man walking to the woods and eventually inside the trees only to disappear entirely have been reported. He doesn't seem to acknowledge anyone or anything. He simply appears, walks into the woods, and vanishes without any indication he was ever there at all. What makes him stand out is the traditional Native American attire he wears and the fact that he's always seen around 7 o'clock at night.

Does the baseball field mark where his home used to be? Or is it something more sacred? He is believed to be more of a residual haunting, less to do with the surroundings around him now and more with that used to be there. He doesn't acknowledge the change, but he does turn to look behind him at least once, as though looking over his shoulder.

Boston Hill Cemetery

Around a grassy knoll of land is a cemetery known as Boston Hill. Named after its generous benefactor, Butler Boston, who donated five acres of his own land for the settlement to use in the late 1880s, Boston Hill became one of the first predominately African American settlements in Oviedo. The five acres became what is now known as Boston Hill Cemetery.

It is in Boston Hill Cemetery that the figure of a man hanging from a tree is seen, sometimes swaying in a wind that isn't actually there. Below his feet is a woman, often seen weeping and praying simultaneously. Was this man a victim of a lynching, or another abominable hate crime? It's unclear who he or the woman might be, only that they appear the same way every time.

Also, the sounds of footsteps in the tall grass is more common than not, and if you look closely enough, the imprints of footsteps can be seen around the grass. Eerily enough, the footsteps will run right up behind a person and then stop as soon as that person turns around. Once they turn back to resume their pace, the footsteps come around again, and again, until the visitor leaves.

And, pockets of fog-like orbs are seen around the actual graves, some of them dating to the founding of Boston Hill itself. The orbs stay in one place, spinning before disappearing, but are often felt even after they've gone. Cold spots litter the hollow ground, remarkably unusual on the sticky and humid Florida days and nights. While no one has been hurt there, or even touched, it's still *not* the most welcoming cemetery to go into after hours.

7

A Ghostly Inhabitant

Super 8 Motel's Room 206

For some places, the number "13" is taboo and not mentioned, for others, there is no room 666 simply for the implications that number carries. In Stephen King's realm, no one wants to get stuck with room 408; but for a small Super 8 Motel located off of International Drive in Orlando (yes, the same highway that has a quarter mile of road known as the Dead Zone), the room number to avoid is "206."

It is in room 206 that a good night's rest is impossible to get. An imprint of a person's body is seen through the newly made covers over the bed; even when the bed is occupied by a guest, often times they will feel someone getting into bed with them.

Alarmed, even if the guest stays perfectly still, the bed has been reported to shake and bounce violently. The room itself is almost frigidly cold, even if the air is turned off and the windows are cracked open to let the Florida heat in. Nothing seems to alleviate the temperature.

When the room itself is quiet, the feeling of being constantly watched cannot be shaken. The bathroom isn't free of the haunting either; the sink will often turn on and off sporadically throughout the day and night. No one can give a name to the spirit who haunts this room—only that a male figure has been seen rising from the bed, only to disappear a moment later after his feet touch the carpet. Was he a traveler, a tourist…or someone who came to the motel to end his life?

There hasn't been any indication of a man ending his life in this motel, so who is the mysterious and slightly intrusive spirit? There's no end to the amount of mystery Orlando's ghosts may bring, however my recommendation would be to avoid room 206 if at all possible, unless of course, a haunted evening is what you came for.

Republican Bank

Haunted bathrooms aren't uncommon in folklore and legend; many town locals can name a few nightclubs with a few haunted bathrooms, faces that appear, and apparitions who lock stalls and doors, leaving frantic patrons banging to get out. What exactly is it about bathrooms that draw ghosts? Many paranormal experts speculate that the site where the bathrooms stand now used to be something else…an office, even a living room before it was torn down and renovated?

It's easier to explain away a school bathroom haunting; children can use a visit to the bathroom as a temporary escape to stretch their legs and break up the monotony of a six-hour school day. But a bank?

In Brevard County, many strange occurrences at a local clubhouse and attached bank has employees and customers alike wondering if the place isn't haunted. Shadowy figures walking up and down the hallways and strange noises when all is quiet is the least of the problem.

Walking into the ladies room, reports of seeing a face in the ladies room mirror above the sinks isn't an everyday occurrence, but it certainly isn't new either. Every couple of weeks, quite a few customers, not knowing the bank's reputation, will come up to an employee and complain about a leering woman, grimacing at them from over their shoulders. The employees, of course, go in there; sometimes they find nothing.

But others...they find more than they want to. A face, sometimes attached to a body, sometimes simply staring at them through the glass will appear for a few moments, glaring. Almost before the mind has time to register what the eyes have just seen, the woman's face is gone without a trace, leaving behind no footsteps, no sound, and no explanation.

But employees and patrons will tell you this is not how it was when they were in there, insisting there *was* a face. Leaning over to fix her makeup in the mirror after using the facilities, one bank patron was surprised to see the face of a woman looking at her. Of course, she turned around to see if the other lady needed to use the mirror as well. But when the patron turned her back to the mirror, there was no one to be found. Unnerved by the woman's sudden disappearance, the patron made to leave. When she turned back to finish packing her purse back up, the woman's image was there in the mirror again, seen from her shoulders and up, staring at the other woman as though she were standing right behind the patron.

The patron fled the bathroom, unsure of how to even explain what just happened to her. *A woman was there, then gone, and there again, all without making a single, solitary sound, just staring at her from over her shoulder.*

No one knows the woman's name or where she comes from. Downtown Orlando, including Brevard County, is full of buildings that used to be historic homes. Was this bank one of them? Was its restroom once someone's living room or bedroom? Many spirits don't recognize when something has changed, and now their bedroom is another building entirely. Is this spirit confused and frustrated, or merely angry?

While no one has reported any sounds or threatening feelings in the bank's restroom, the face in the mirror is definitely a more unsettling experience. And it's not even the only experience that's been told. Doors will open with no one there to push or turn the knob, and elevators will open and shut several times; no one will be there, but the sounds of footsteps will echo around before dissipating into silence.

There's even been the sighting of a shadowy figure moving in between doorways and offices. It's faceless, nameless, and no one can tell if it's a man or a woman apparition, but it's there. Could it be the same face that manifests in the bathroom? Or are there several spirits still hanging around the Citrus Center bank?

Miller, Sellen, Conner, & Walsh Law Office

It almost sounds like the beginning of a bad joke. Hey, did you hear the one about the law office that was haunted? But in the case of the Miller, Sellen, Conner, & Walsh law office, it's no joke: it's true. Former and current employees speak about what goes on in the office when, near the end of the day, not many other people are about...like voices echoing down the hallway that don't answer when you call out "Who's there?" One former employee recalls getting up and down several times from his desk chair to look out in the hallway after inquiring who was out there. Over and over again, snippets of voices would float in and out of his hearing range until the worker finally decided it was just time to go home. The eerie feeling of not being alone when no one else is about is too much to handle, and happens often.

Another such employee described how he got a call on his phone from another office extension. But when he picked up the phone, there was only static on the other end, and, filtering through the static, the sound of a child playing and laughing, faint but persistent. He was, again, the only person in the office.

The sound of someone who isn't there running down the hallways isn't exceptional, either. Of course, when an employee walks out to meet the expectant runner, there's no one there and the running footsteps taper off into silence. It happens numerous times a day, usually when only a few employees are left. The shy spirit seems to come out after hours, but not necessarily after dark. This haunting seems to depend on the amount of people in the vicinity, *not* the time of day.

The building that the Miller, Sellen, Conner, & Walsh Law Office now resides in doesn't look like your run-of-the-mill haunted location, but in fact, is an old historic building dating back to the early 1900s. Originally used as a family's home, the site was declared historic and therefore, safe from the threat of being torn down. While phantom phone calls and the pitter-patter of invisible footsteps may seem a bit creepy, the atmosphere as a whole doesn't seem to be frightening or malevolent. Moreover, the feeling the building seems to give off is confused, almost as if whatever, or whoever, is there isn't quite sure what's going on. Isn't this house still their house?

Perhaps with time, this haunting will make itself more well known, satisfying curious questions of who's haunting the building, and what do they want.

8

The Grandparents' Tale

My Grandmother's Story

In 1979, my grandmother, Elizabeth Lieble, moved to Central Florida to a small, undeveloped portion of East Orange County with her second husband, Frank Lieble Jr. Trying to incorporate themselves into Orlando life, they often attended civic meetings where people in the immediate area would get together and discuss community news.

On one such occasion in 1981, my grandmother remembered the topic of an elderly lady, a Ms. Brolyn, and her home, coming up in concern.

"I can't even recall her first name, I only knew her as Ms. Brolyn. She was an older lady, and she lived over in town, near Econ Trail. The community was trying to get her to leave her house, said it was dirty and real unsafe. She lived there all by herself; no one could ever recall anyone ever entering the house, or anyone ever leaving.

"She refused to leave the house. Outright refused."

According to my grandmother, when she was asked if she didn't get lonely being all alone in the house, Mrs. Brolyn replied, "I'm never alone." It was an earlier time for Orlando, where there were more cow pastures than neighborhoods. Most of the "neighborhoods" around were more like smaller streets with homes clustered about, off of Colonial Drive, hardly in the suburbia boom that would come in later years. Ms. Brolyn lived in a section of town used for small government subsidized homes; something that at one time had looked pretty, but had fallen into disrepair over the years. It became a forlorn-looking place, needing more upkeep than it was worth. The thought was to eventually tear the homes down and sell the space cheap for offices in the growing town of Orlando.

According to my grandmother, a small corner store kept Ms. Brolyn fed and delivered all her meals to her doorstep. "I don't think she paid them, I think it was something the owners just did. It was one of those older mom-and-pop sort of place. They probably felt bad for her, living like she did.

"It was about four weeks after the community meeting that she took ill and died in her house. I don't know who, maybe the corner store people, but somebody called the police, concerned."

Used to calls concerning elderly people living by themselves, the police did go to the dilapidated house. While they were unsurprised to find Ms. Brolyn deceased, they were surprised by something else.

"She was all dressed," my grandmother recalled, "dressed and ready for the casket. Someone had bathed her, clothed her, and laid her out. Of course, when they took her body away, they had to do an autopsy, make sure it was a natural death." The paper said that the coroner reported that she *had* died a natural death, but that she had died probably about forty-eight hours before the police found her. The police said she looked like she had died maybe a few hours before they arrived. No one knew who dressed her, or if she had somehow known she was close to death and simply dressed herself.

Nothing more was thought of Ms. Brolyn until the demolition to her house started. Without a will or next of kin to claim the house, the city auctioned it off; it was only when the demolition and refurbishing of the house began that people remembered

Ms. Brolyn and her constant answer to their incessant questions about being lonely or needing help.

I'M NEVER ALONE.

Right away, things started going wrong with the construction. Machines broke and all sorts of accidents happened. Some of the workers just up and quit and ran off, leaving their equipment there for the next set of people to find. They all said they heard voices, some of them demanding that the workers leave; it got so bad and so frequent that the newspaper ran a story about the haunted house. "I read about it in the paper myself," my grandmother shook her head. "But she always said that it was *her* house and that she was taken care of." Eventually, the city maintenance managed to tear down the house. They tried to sell the land off for office buildings and other commercial uses, but no one ever bought the land plot either; the reputation of a claimed haunted house was enough warning.

Sipping her coffee, my grandmother held her hands up. "I don't know what was in that house, but I can tell you this: whatever it was, she wasn't ever alone, and no one could ever stay in that plot of land for more than a few days. And that's all I can tell you."

It's hard to locate the plot of land that still stays vacant, and even harder to imagine that a growing place like Orlando, Florida would purposely not use a supposedly perfectly fine space of land. But not so hard to imagine if you believe the story that Ms. Brolyn was never alone.

My Grandfather's Story

I imagine life wouldn't have been very fair if my grandmother had a story to tell about a ghostly experience, but my grandfather, Frank, did not. This one, though, I was present for.

In 1990, we got a new neighbor named Jack. He was an older gentleman, a few years older than my grandfather. I don't know what he did for a living, but he didn't seem to ever leave his house. He and my grandfather hit it off; they both liked to keep busy, they liked lawn mowers, stained glass, and basic home repair. They had a fairly good, genial friendship, lasting even after my grandparents left to live in West Virginia for a few years before returning back to Florida.

Jack became older, like all people. When I went away to college, he became sick, but instead of getting better, he seemed to go on a fast decline. My grandfather was often called to help him in some way.

It was at this time that Jack's two daughters came down to see about their father; this surprised us all. We had no idea he even had daughters, they hadn't been to see Jack at all. My grandfather was the one who helped Jack. They didn't stay too long, and after they left, my grandfather returned to taking care of Jack.

When he died, my grandfather, Frank, was the one who called the hospital and took care of things, until Jack daughters came back to finish up the estate. It was probably about three days after the funeral; I was home for the evening, working late on a couple of projects. It wasn't an all-nighter, but it was close: 3:20 a.m. was when I finally went to bed. Thankful that I didn't have class or work the following day, I went to sleep.

I woke up to the sound of my grandparents bringing in the groceries, and stumbled out to help them, but the blinking red light from their answering machine caught my eye.

"You guys have a message," I said, and hit the play button on my way to put the milk away.

My grandmother and my grandfather both paused. The mechanical voice chirped out, "One new message on Saturday, 2:17 a.m."

There was a pause for a moment, and then a confused sounding voice came through the speakers. "...Frank? Listen, it's Jack. Frank, I need your help. I don't know where I am, but... well, I'll just try you later."

It *was* Jack's voice coming out of the speakers, unmistakably his. Years of living side by side, my grandfather could probably pick out two voices in this life without fail: Jack's and my grandmother's. "Frank? Frank, what is this?" My grandmother looked around wildly as though the house would give her an answer. My grandfather and I, for our part, just stared at the answering machine.

I licked my lips. "Maybe this isn't the best time, but I was up until 3 a.m. The phone never rang."

For a moment, we thought maybe the time was off, somehow, so I called the house line from my cell phone. But when we replayed that message, it gave us the correct date and time.

We never got another phone message from Jack, but I have often looked next door, to the new family that moved into Jack's house and wonder if anything unusual has happened in there. Jack did sound very confused, after all.

9

Leu Botanical Gardens

††††††††††

**1920 North Forest Avenue,
Orlando, Florida 32803**

††††††††††

In high school, many field trips were taken to Leu Gardens, for just about any reason. To practice drawing our plants and scenery more realistically, the Art Club took us all to Leu Gardens for a day. To learn more about botany in their natural setting, our Biology teacher took us to Leu Gardens. To practice naming plant life and different species of birds, we went on a field trip to Leu Gardens, and had there been a cooking club, we probably would have ended up at Leu Gardens to study how herbs and spices are grown in their natural habitat.

No one really thought about the Gardens being haunted; in fact, if I were to choose which area in Orlando surprised me the most about having a haunted reputation, I would have to pick Leu Gardens. It's serene and peaceful there, with more than just pretty flowers. Bamboo stalks tower overhead, cacti by the dozen gather in close groups of nettles and flesh stalks, and there's even a real working clock made out of different plants and flowers, the hands pointing to the correct hour and minute.

Harry P. Leu was the last and final owner of the turn-of-the-century mansion on the property now known as Leu Botanical Gardens. An Orlando native, Leu was born on June 11, 1884, and bought the deed to the mansion and surrounding property in 1936. When he married later on in years, he and his lovely wife, Mary Jane, traveled all over the world, collecting exotic roses, over 240 breeds of camellias, cacti, and herbs. They traveled by boat, plane, ox cart, car, bus, and even elephant to find these plants and make his grounds beautiful. No matter how far the pair traveled, or how long they were gone, they always returned to their home in Orlando.

After a time, Leu and his wife decided that all of Orlando should be able to enjoy their massive gardens as much as they did and opened the grounds for the public to come and tour through their gardens.

In 1961, Leu gave the deed to the mansion and the gardens over to the city of Orlando, wanting to give something back to the city where he had made his fortune and spent the happiest years of his life. So happy, in fact, that visitors and tour guides claim he and his wife haven't left their mansion yet.

Guided tours of the Leu are given daily, to show what life was like right before the twentieth century. But all is not just historical fact on these twenty-minute tours. The house, which has since been turned into a museum, has been told to have lingering snippets of spirits. Activities and phenomena have been reported; cold spots in the upper bedrooms are what tourists usually will remark on.

Of course, a house built in 1906 had no central air and heating, and it has not been changed to include such modernizations. Much of how the house was when it was first built has been restored, but still many people will report on how *icy cold* it is in some portions of the upper bedrooms, odd for a house located in the middle of Florida.

What the tourists don't see – but the tour guides *do* – are actual spirits, walking and roaming the mansion. They seem to be at peace though; whereas most spirits may cringe and balk at the idea of strangers entering their house, Leu and his wife were more than open about letting the citizens of Orlando view and enjoy their home and their gardens.

Footsteps with no one there to make them are often heard up on the second-story porch, strolling along almost at a meandering pace. Humming and soft voices are said to be heard around the sprawling mansion, without anyone there to be making them, and every so often, a tour guide sees the solid manifestation of a spirit.

Interestingly enough, the museum tours given to schoolchildren are conducted by a volunteer dressed up in period costume. There, the guide takes the children around the house and explains what life was like when they "lived" there. Once, a tour guide, wrapping up for the afternoon, thought she saw a person dressed in period costume and appearing to get ready for a tour. But, the tours were over at 3:30 in the afternoon and it was already well past 4 o'clock. When she went over to the young woman to explain that work for the day was over and that she could get ready to go home, the other woman smiled and vanished...as though not ever having been there at all.

If the spirits bother the caretakers of Leu Botanical Gardens, you wouldn't know it from their activities; most Octobers, one evening is set aside for an event where ghost stories are told right outside, near the museum. I wonder if Leu and his wife are participants?

10

Sunland Hospital

M any people are well aware of Sunland Hospital, sometimes referred to as "Sunnyland," in Tallahassee, Florida. The hospital, now closed, is reportedly haunted with a high volume of spirits of children. But what people don't know is that Sunland Hospital is actually a branch of hospitals that started right here in Orlando, Florida.

Long before Orlando became synonymous with theme parks and smiles of little children and adults alike, it was a veritable nightmare for anyone to be sent to Orlando. In the mid 1940s, the Sunland Hospital branch opened, the first in its chain as a tuberculosis quarantine center, also known as the W. T. Edwards Center. Children of all ages were sent to the hospital for treatment and quarantine until they were well again.

Rumors of patients being mistreated at this clinic abounded, but was never able to be proven. Patients died, and if anyone questioned the nature of the children's death, it was chalked up to their disease and not mistreatment. They may not have been buried on the hospital site, but that was where many of them died, and, so it is told, their spirits remain in anguish where their living bodies had been so sick.

In 1963, the threat of tuberculosis subsided and Sunland Hospital closed down until 1965, when it reopened as the Sunland Training Center of Orlando for mentally and physically handicapped children and adults. If there were any reports of haunted activity from the prior usage of the building, it was most likely written off as untrue babbling from the poor patients. Staff members ignored any stories, and the poor treatment of patients continued as it had before.

Many handicapped children and adults were dropped off at the center by their families, some believing their children were getting a good education, others to simply be rid of their handicapped family members. Despite rumors of abuse mounting, concerns were brushed aside.

In 1967, the Sunland Hospital chain opened its center in Tallahassee and eighteen patients were relocated to become the first Tallahassee patients, though the conditions were not much improved. Stories of electroshock therapy and an uncaring and morally loose staff—one female patient was said to have been impregnated by a staff member—were some of the nightmarish ways of life for these patients. Children were being housed in the same areas as some of the more violent patients with no boundaries or healthy dividers between the two. Eventually it was harder to keep the stories of rampant abuse and blatant disregard for the health and well being of the patients quiet and, as more examples of mistreatment came to light, both the Orlando and Tallahassee Sunland Hospitals came under close scrutiny. Plans to shut down the hospitals were underway, and in 1983 both the Orlando and Tallahassee centers were closed.

Until 1997, the Orlando structure remained standing. Reports of a haunted building were not far behind the initial closing in 1983. Lights that could not be explained away appeared, and sounds were heard that were not being made by anyone alive. Footsteps made by unseen little legs were seen in the dust and, rusty, left-over beds were reported to have been moved all on their own, blocking groups of curious people in particular rooms.

Groups of people flocked to the abandoned hospital in Orlando. Toys were brought in and said to have been moved and played with. Sounds of a child jumping rope in the ward above a group of unofficial tourists were frequent, as well as sounds of objects being dropped and even thrown from far across the fetid floors of the now-abandoned building. Tales of ghost children seen jumping on their beds, as well as stories of groups being cornered in examination rooms where they suddenly found doors that had worked before, closed and locked, blocking their pathways out of said room came frequently.

But these accounts did little to ward off other illegal visitors to the abandoned building...once the spirit of a little boy was seen on the upper levels, frantically searching for something, ducking between hallways and doorways. It is said he then paused, looked at the small group of people watching him, and continued on his search.

Another, slightly more chilling sighting at the abandoned Sunland Hospital was that of a young girl, sitting at the landing of the third floor staircase. The young girl apparition was sighted screaming silently in absolute terror before hurling herself off the landing and down the stairs...before she simply disappeared. The third floor ward of the Orlando Sunland Hospital was locked, inexplicably, and no wayward explorer could ever get it open. Was this why the young spirit was so upset? No one will ever know now.

Despite the dilapidated structure, the graffiti that labeled the walls, and a thick infestation of asbestos mold, the building was well-visited, and the signs proclaiming "Do Not Enter" and "No Trespassing" were ignored. Until 1997, when an ill-fated visitor went through what he thought was another pair of doors, but actually turned out to be a broken down elevator shaft. He fell three stories, suffering a fractured skull and several injuries to his back and spine.

While the ill-fated visitor survived his fall, the incident prompted nearby residents to push for the structure to finally be torn down. It was, and in its place, a playground was constructed. But just because the building is gone, does not mean the ghosts have gone away with it.

Reports of swings going to and fro by themselves at full force and sounds of children by the slide when there is no one there, gives evidence that just because the sanatorium is gone does not mean the spirits do not still remain. This could be considered a happy ending for the spirits of tortured patients—a playground replacing their own personal hell on earth? Maybe it will help them move on, the bit of playtime they never got while alive.

Greenwood Cemetery, one of the largest in Orlando, has a section devoted entirely to the residents of Sunland Hospital, grave markers worn away by weather and age. I went there to further my research—that experience will be shared in a different section.

11

The Annie Russell Theatre

†††††††††††

**1000 Holt Avenue – 2735 Winter Park, Florida 32789-4499
in Rollins College.**

†††††††††††

ollins College has good reason to state that its college is one of the finest private colleges in Florida—its MBA program was one of the first in Central Florida, the campus is beautiful and easy to navigate, and the college can even boast of having its own ghost.

The Annie Russell Theatre was built in honor of actress Annie Russell, one of the first prolific ladies on the stage. A native of Liverpool, England, Annie Russell was born in 1864 to Irish parents. The family moved to Canada when Annie was still a small child, and soon the vibrant little girl found her calling to the stage. At Montreal's Academy of Music, Annie made her first stage appearance at the prolifically young age of eight years old. After a brief acting stint in the West Indies when she was twelve, the well-traveled, talented young actress moved to New York when she was still a teenager. At seventeen, the charming, doe-eyed young Annie landed a role in the play "Esmeralda," launching her career into full force. Her delicate beauty and strong voice let all who saw her know that Annie Russell was no passing star—she would be noticed and she would be grand. She had the drive and the energy, despite frequent, sometimes long-winded illnesses that forced her to lay low for periods of time.

In 1918, the older, yet no less graceful, actress officially retired from the stage and moved to Winter Park, Florida. She was urged by a friend to teach at Rollins College, and did so in 1932, opening the Annie Russell Theatre. There she taught classes, imparting her experience and her wisdom of the stage to her students. In her later years, Annie spent much of her time teaching and giving speeches to other hopeful drama students; it seemed the lady of the stage had no shortage of time to devote to other would-be stars.

On February 25, 1936, Annie Russell's star dimmed as the actress passed away from an illness of the lungs; she was seventy-two years old.

But the story doesn't end there. Many students and faculty members will testify that Annie is still in her theatre, watching over productions of plays. Helpful until the end, and then beyond the end, Annie seems to favor her small theatre where so many actors and actresses were educated by her, and after her.

One such story of Annie's spirit still staying on the campus involves her chair; while living and directing shows at Rollins, Annie had her own chair she used to watch rehearsals from and give critiques. It was always in the same spot. And to this very day, Annie has her own chair that, no matter how many times it is moved away, is moved back to her spot during rehearsals. Several times, actors have paused, just to hear the rattling and banging of the chair being pushed back into position, and they know Annie is taking note of their performance.

Phantom clapping is also heard, a bit of ghostly encouragement the closer opening night draws near, near the back of the theatre seats. A bust statue of Annie's head and face has been erected in her honor in the small stage-house, which is also seen moving slowly across the theatre.

A well-known story of Annie's benevolent spirit is that of a student working late hours at the theatre before a play was set to open the next night. Working alone on the light grid, the student was perched precariously on a ladder while he checked and double-checked the light gels used in the performance. He leaned too far forward and found himself tumbling down below, landing hard on the ground. Injured, the student couldn't move, could not call out for help; everyone else had gone home for the evening, or so he thought.

Several minutes went by before someone peeked into the curiously open theatre – later on, no one could recall leaving the door open at all – to see the injured student laying there. They rushed to call an ambulance, only be informed by the 911 operator that they had already been alerted to the injured student and help was on its way. Sure enough, an ambulance arrived within moments to take the fallen student to the hospital.

Who left the doors open, and who called the ambulance? No one has ever stepped forward to claim the heroism that happened that night, and the injured student, who made a full recovery, swore he was completely alone with the doors not only shut, but locked from the inside. Most will tell anyone who asks that it was Annie, still teaching and still helping "her" students to this very day.

12

Living with a Ghost

Player's Park, part 1

It's safe to assume every writer who writes about the paranormal has had their own experience with things that creep around staircases at night. Close encounters with what we cannot explain often drive us to explore it and reach out to others who have had their own experiences. Many people find solace in this, and feel free to let go of whatever experience unnerved them, and go on to live normal, productive lives.

Then there are the ones who never let go and commence to write an entire book about ghosts.

I suppose it's easy to see which category I fall into.

Before I turned eighteen, the closest experience with the paranormal I ever had was with various horror novels, episodes of "Unsolved Mysteries," and my mother's story of sensing her deceased father's spirit and his disapproval of her current boyfriend after he passed away, a feeling that lay over their small apartment in New York that didn't leave until she broke up with said, unapproved boyfriend. If you had honestly asked me then if I really believed in haunted houses, I would have truthfully told you I probably didn't. And if I did, I thought them to be old, historic homes, like the kind Robert Stack faithfully reported on, or where battles of war and bloodshed had been, or even a drafty castle or two. But a townhouse in the middle of Central Florida, built in the mid-1980s, would not have been my idea of a haunted living space.

Right after I graduated from high school, my mother, Michele, and I moved out of the apartment we had been renting and into a rent-to-own townhouse built in the mid-1980s, located right off of State Road 436. The complex contained a cluster of these older, yet still nice-looking townhouses called Player's Park. The first time our real estate agent showed us around, the townhouse seemed beautiful and quaint, and fairly modern despite its twenty-plus year age. It was larger than the apartment, but not too big. It was close to the college campus I would be attending in the fall, and as I was on scholarship that didn't include living in a dorm, and didn't have the money to move out, I was staying home until I could save enough money.

It seemed ideal. Every appliance including the refrigerator and air conditioning had just been replaced, the carpets freshly cleaned, and for once, the walls were painted different colors, rather than the plain white I was used to. We made an offer and later that day, the owner quickly accepted. The townhouse was ours.

It seemed to go the way of every dream-home story...*until* we actually moved in.

The townhouse was two-stories, with the ground floor including two double-sliding glass doors and a regular front door located in a miniature courtyard with stunted palm trees around. Family, friends, and their children were kind enough to help us move, so as we started unloading the moving van, we had all agreed the fastest way to get the boxes in and get us out of the sticky, Florida heat would be to leave the door and both sliding glass doors open and everyone to work as an assembly line, emptying out the van and depositing all the boxes downstairs.

As we commenced moving the boxes inside, all went smoothly for the first few minutes until I heard a booming crash from inside the courtyard. Karen, my mother's friend, and myself jumped out of the van, leaving our boxes to find Aaron, Karen's twelve-year-old son, sprawled on the ground, box toppled over, the glass door shut. He was hysterical, pointing at the door.

"It closed on me!
IT just closed
... and I ran into *it!"*

Picking him up, his mother and I checked for injuries while the others crowded around him, insisting that the door had probably been closed by accident by one of the guys inside. No one remembered closing the door, but what other explanation could there be? Aaron persisted the rest of the day, claiming he saw the door slide shut in front of him, too quickly to allow him to stop going forward. We chalked it up to pre-teen pride and finished the rest of the day without incident.

After the customary pizza for supper, our friends and family left with Aaron still insisting the door closed on him. We didn't think anything of it, until my mother and I noticed the townhouse was still very warm inside. Checking the air conditioner, my mother found it running, but no air was being pumped inside.

It puzzled both of us, as the air conditioner had just been replaced. Having no choice but to call in a repair service, my mother and I settled down to sleep, but something felt...off. Eager for a reason why I felt uncomfortable in our chaotic, but new home, I blamed the heat and slept with the door open. The bedrooms and bathrooms were upstairs while the laundry room, kitchen, living, and dining areas were downstairs, but both bedrooms, since they were upstairs, had sliding glass doors for windows.

When we moved, we had brought everything, including the budgie bird, Toby. He was a small bird, but active and as hyper and happy as most small birds are. Hardly a morning went by at the apartment that didn't begin the day with Toby chirping, singing, or just plain screeching. But on his new perch in my room, he didn't make a peep. In the morning, I came down for breakfast, mentioning it to my mother, but she and I both assumed it was the move and new location; when he got used to the new room, he'd start singing again. But he never did. We lived there for six months, five months of living there and one month to sell the place, but Toby *never* made a sound the entire time.

In the first few weeks my mother and I lived in the townhouse, a myriad of repairs had to be made. As soon as one appliance had been replaced, something else broke, and the cycle would start all over again. When I looked at the receipts, it shocked me and disheartened my mother and I to discover what we were replacing was only months old. Why was everything suddenly breaking? Odder still, the humidity bags we kept in each of our closets, designed to collect and keep out the added moisture in the air from our clothes, needed to be replaced bi-weekly. The plastic, two-gallon bags filled up with water quickly, in less than half the time they should have, leaving us baffled. They were small things, but they added up.

Even with the air conditioning replaced, the townhouse continued to emit an uncomfortable heat, leaving both my mother and I snappish and on edge. The place itself felt weird. It just felt "bad," as weak a word as that may be, and it made people uncomfortable. We would only start laughing and joking again once we went out on errands, or to school and work. But inside, it was really tense, so much so that we started sighing in a "here we go again" type of way.

Things went missing. At first, it was my mother's sewing needles. She came into my room one night as I read. "Hey hun, did you take my sewing needles?"

"No, I didn't." I didn't need to, I had my own. But, instead of saying this calmly, we both started to fight, *really* fight with vehemence.

Despite knowing I had my own and hadn't been in her room at all that day, my mother became annoyed. "Well, they're gone, so where did they go?"

"Geez, Mom, I don't know, but I didn't take them! I have my own stupid needles."

Even as we argued and fought, it didn't sound right. We'd had our arguments in the past, but never over trivial things like this. It was scary how worked up we became over what began as a simple question. The next day, my cell phone went missing, then the kitchen scissors, my extra sewing fabric, my mother's candles, new paint cans, and the next week, wall paper we were thinking of using in the dining room. Shaken by our fight, we didn't ask each other again where anything else went; we simply started to look for them, finding, of course, nothing.

Before college classes started in the fall, the routine for the mornings started with my mother leaving for work, and myself slogging downstairs to the living room. I had taken the summer off after graduating high school in an accelerated program, the first summer off in four years. No job, no extra classes, and no summer reading... It seemed like bliss to wake up and watch television before calling up friends to hang out.

A month and a half after we moved in, I started hearing voices downstairs, near the kitchen and dining room. One morning, figuring the voice meant my mom hadn't left yet, I bounded downstairs to see what the delay was.

No one was there. I called out, even though I could see the entire layout of the room from where I stood by the stairs. I was literally the only person in the house. Shaken, but convinced maybe I was (somehow) hearing the neighbors through the walls and the floor, I sat down on the couch directly in front of the television. I kept it off as I strained to hear something else...something to explain the voices. I shifted in my seat, and turned, facing the television. As I was about to turn it on, I could hear a slow, scraping sound from the counter behind me in the kitchen. I froze, listening to the deliberate sound as it suddenly became faster, and something was sent clattering to the floor. I whirled around to see my glasses that I had left downstairs the night before (I usually wore my contact lenses first thing in the morning) had been sent flying on the floor, scratched but otherwise unharmed. By this time, I wasn't sure I *wanted* to know where the voices were coming from.

Clutching my battered glasses, I sat back down on the couch. My heart was pounding, and I couldn't really process what I had just heard. I turned and saw my reflection from the turned-off television staring back at me, but from behind the couch, behind me, I saw a figure move, walking from one end of the room to the other.

It was a woman, clearly older than I, in a long dress, with long dark hair that was left free and unbound, all the way to her back. The dress looked old fashioned, but I couldn't begin classifying which time period it was from. Though it happened in a matter of a few seconds, I will never forget seeing that woman quickly walking from one end of the room to the other, disappearing into the wall.

It was a moment that filled me so acutely with terror I couldn't even move for a minute; I sat in shock until I forced my legs to move to run out the door with the cordless phone and called my grandfather. I waited for him in my pajamas, not caring that every motorist pulling into the townhouse complex could probably see me and would more than likely think I was an escaped mental patient for waiting on the side of the road barefoot and in my robe. I called him to come and get me; I was not staying there. Which in hindsight was probably what "she," whomever she was, wanted.

Player's Park, part II

The same night I saw the woman, I sat in bed, feeling foolish. My grandfather checked the entire upstairs and downstairs and other than discovering a crawl space we hadn't known was there before, nothing came up. No ladies, no broken glass to suggest a break-in, nothing in there but a couple of boxes we had yet to unpack.

Of course, I told my mother as soon as she got home. If I didn't, my grandfather would, or (and this seemed even worse) what happened downstairs with the woman walking through the wall could happen again. To my surprise, my mother didn't sound very skeptical at my story at all. But she had had her own experiences that she didn't share with me until after we moved out. While we didn't want to tell anyone about what was going on in the house, my seeing the woman's reflection in the television was the very last straw.

The upstairs consisted of our bedrooms, and the second bathroom down a narrow hall that sat right on the edge of the stairwell. My mother brought a hallway nightlight in case we ever had to get up in the middle of the night, to ensure neither one of us tumbled down the stairs. Her nightly routine consisted of grabbing her robe, and on her way to the bathroom to wash up, plugging in the nightlight and turning it on. The trouble started immediately.

Coming out of the bathroom drying her face, she noticed the nightlight wasn't in the wall. Strange, she thought, because she was sure she had plugged it in. Upon going back in her room, my mother found the nightlight unplugged and placed in the middle of her bed. During the day when it wasn't in use, she stored it in her nightstand by her dresser. Figuring she had simply forgot it, my mother shrugged it off and re-plugged it in the wall, where it stayed the rest of the evening.

Convinced the previous night was her own mistake, my mother didn't think anything of it as she went in to wash up for bed, plugging the hall nightlight in as she went. But again, as she came out and went to her room, the nightlight was not in the wall socket, but was sitting in the middle of her bed. Her first thought was that I was doing it, before she realized I wasn't home that particular evening as I was out with friends.

Again, for a third night, she went in to wash, plugged the nightlight in the socket, and once more, she found it unplugged and sitting in the middle of her bed. This night, she had even paused to stare at the nightlight for a minute before going in to wash her face. But like every other night, it ended up unplugged, in the middle of her bed.

At night, things seemed to move around a lot. The computer refused to stay connected to the Internet and would randomly turn on and off during the night and day. One evening, after I started college in August, I had stayed up late finishing a report for my World History class. As I printed out the last paper, I turned everything off and headed for bed. What happened next seemed like slow motion; as I bent my arm to move the white stuffed tiger I received as a graduation present, the stuffed animal wiggled a moment before being flung across the room by unseen hands. I was still two feet away from the actual bed, and I froze, my arm still extended before slowly backing away and sleeping on the floor with the lights on.

It was time to ask Pastor Paul to bless the townhouse. But how do you call up your very kind yet down-to-earth Pastor and ask him to bless your new home because you thought it was haunted?

Wriggling stuffed tigers and breaking appliances aside, the entire house felt abnormal. Pressing down on us, my mother and I both knew without saying as much aloud that whatever was in the townhouse did not want us in it either. The feeling of playful tricks and feeding from our apparent discomfort didn't make us feel physically threatened, per se, but we knew the overall atmosphere was screaming at us to get out. We weren't wanted.

Even my grandmother came forward after we told the family we were getting the townhouse blessed and told us it was a good idea. Like my mother and myself, she kept quiet, feeling foolish for believing in ghosts. She told us she heard someone racing up and down the stairs, laughing, as she sat in the dining room. She had gone over to the bottom of the staircase, thinking it was my younger cousin, Madison, and I racing up and down. She called up, "That's not a very good idea, you should know better than to teach Madison that!" Going back to her seat, my grandmother again heard the sound of racing feet up and down the stairs. She turned back to call out another annoyed warning until she caught sight of my younger cousin and I sweeping the fallen pine needles from the patio. No one else was in the townhouse but her.

Even my Aunt Lisa had a story about the townhouse; before we moved in, she and my mother had gone to the townhouse to pick up some extra packing material the previous owner hadn't used, but offered us the leftovers. It was a nice offer, and we took her up on it, but when my aunt and mother went to get the extra boxes and newspaper, they found the newspaper and bubble wrap shredded and tossed around the carpet; it looked like an animal had gotten to it. We knew the lady had a dog and figured the pet had gone on a rampage without the owner knowing about it, but now, we weren't so sure it was done by anything living. *Paranoid, now everything that made a bang, every lost sock, had a paranormal origin to it—every shadow was the woman coming back*. We couldn't live like that.

Our pastor was glad to come bless the townhouse, but even so, we all kept our fears and suspicions and stories to ourselves, even though we were all entirely convinced something was wrong with the townhouse. The blessing commenced, and the minute Pastor Paul left, the house felt lighter, felt normal. It alarmed us; we hadn't known just how bad we felt in the townhouse until we had something to compare it to. And for a few weeks, it felt better—*it felt like a REGULAR home should*. Even though my bird, Toby, still didn't make a sound, it was less scary being there, especially alone and at night. The air wasn't heavy, and we were no longer on edge.

It didn't last, however. Soon after, our reprieve was up. This time, there were no flying glasses, or mere shadow reflected in the glass of a television, or footsteps on the stairs. This time it came with unexplained water trickling down the walls and a horrible stench in the mornings. At first, I figured an animal had literally died around the house, or even on top of the roof. But a search provided nothing, no explanations, and no proof.

And we had had enough. November came, and my mother and I decided we'd had enough. No more voices, no more moving objects—we couldn't make *it* go away. Whatever *it* was that was in this townhouse wanted us gone, and we were more than happy to oblige. The financial burden of replacing new, yet somehow broken appliances had drained our finances. The ceiling had water damage from the water that had trickled down the walls, and we literally had no more fight in us to stay. Even if we'd had the money to keep repairing and re-fixing everything, the mood and impression of the townhouse was more than enough.

So, after living in our dream home for a little less than six months, my mother and I moved out. We sold the townhouse to a couple of just-out of college girls, roommates. Unsure of how to advise them, we simply told them to be safe and call us if they had any problems. Before we turned the keys over to them, I said to one, "No, really—call us if you have any problems whatsoever."

They never did call us, but they didn't end up staying very long either, selling the townhouse in a matter of months as well. More than likely, like us, they felt foolish for believing in ghosts and hauntings. We never found out who the lady was or if she was the only one in the house. Were there more? Did they also want us out? My friends will still ask me, with relish, to talk about Player's Park, reminding me NOT to leave out the woman or the floating stuffed animals. It wasn't a sensational haunting; no groaning walls or mysterious blood puddles, but still unexplainable enough to cause alarm. Sometimes, when the nights are warm and I have nothing better to do, I sit in my own home and wonder who owns the townhouse at Player's Park, and if they're having an easier time with it than we did.

13

Church Street Station

I n the 1970s and 1980s, Church Street Station used to be the place to go for the nightlife in Orlando. Clubs, dance halls, themed bars, and shops featuring interesting baked sweets and boasting of "The Ultimate Pizza Experience" were everywhere. Despite the name, Church Street is not just a street, nor is it merely one building, but an area that encases about ten square miles around and in downtown metropolitan Orlando. It consists of many streets filled with just as many businesses aimed at one thing: tourism. Fun was available for all who came, and for a while it was the number one venue for fun after dark. But in the late 1980s and early 1990s, that changed, and with added additions of clubs and shops around the tourist attractions and theme parks, Church Street's entertainment value dropped and was forced to close in 1999.

A revival kicked up the dust and settled ruins of abandoned and closed stores; in late 2007, several old favorites reopened, bringing back new and old businesses to breathe life again into Church Street Station. With a long history and tall tales to go around during reconstruction of the newly re-opened entertainment strip, there was hardly any surprise to ghost hunters and paranormal investigators alike that all the renovating awoke the spirits of Church Street Station as well. It was due for a paint job, anyway, especially since the original Church Street Station was founded and built in 1860.

The main street of Church Street has a definite country-and-cowboy feel to it, despite its religious beginnings. What is now known as Cerviche's Restaurant, a hip musically inclined restaurant where many famous boy bands were discovered, is actually made from the remnants of a cathedral.

In 1860, a priest from Louisiana literally picked up and moved his entire cathedral, piece by piece, to Orlando, Florida, giving Church Street its name. The structure, like much of Church Street, is still standing today, and is still used. In fact, many of the buildings are in their original forms, built in the 1860s through the 1880s. Not only is the original wooden structure still sound and standing, but many of the antiques and artifacts from the original owners and from Orlando's earliest days are there as well. Oh, and some of the original owners and proprietors themselves are still hanging around too.

Church Street Station Train.
This particular train no longer runs of
course, but it makes an impressive
sight on the original tracks.

Cerviche's Restaurant

Other than being the site of the launching careers of boy bands, as previously mentioned, Cerviche's is also the site of many hauntings. A mirror hangs above the bar, an original mirror from the late 1860s, but it's not the mirror that's fascinating... it's the woman who *appears* behind customers, dressed in period clothing. Mistaking the lovely woman in the blouse and flounced skirt as a waitress, she is usually greeted with smiles. Upon turning around, the customers aim to greet the lady and give her their orders, but as soon as they turn from the bar to face her, she's gone, disappearing as though there was no one there at all. Often, the bartenders on duty are asked where the waitress went. "You know, the one in costume!" is often how they describe her. The tender will more often shake their heads and as gently as possible explain to the bewildered costumer that none of the waiters or waitresses wear period costumes in this restaurant.

"But we saw her in the mirror!" They point, but of course, the old mirror just hangs there, giving no sign. No one is sure of her name, or if she was the original owner of the mirror, donated to what used to be a church. But the mysterious woman in the mirror is hardly the only spirit at Cerviche's.

Before it was a restaurant, but after it was a church, the building that now houses Cerviche's used to be a hotel. Renovated from the church in 1922, the Strand Hotel was anything but quiet and sleepy. Several witnesses and overnight guests would claim the hotel was haunted, but few of the workers believed it; accounts of an old man hanging by his neck on the rafters and creaking stairs seemed simply untrue. After all, who believed in ghost stories? The hotel was old and people had overactive imaginations. Despite that even the previous manager had an experience with an otherworldly visitor and left because of it, there were still disbelievers.

The hotel manager had quit because he maintained that he had had an encounter with a ghostly piano player. The piano in the foyer was a regular upright piano, and one evening, the manager was on his way to double-check everything at the front desk. Upon arriving downstairs, the manager heard piano playing and followed the sound. It was well-past midnight and guests were discouraged from playing around on the piano anyway. As the manager entered the foyer, he saw a well-dressed man in a suit with a bowler hat on his head. Frowning, the manager stepped forward and told the man that, while his playing was lovely, it was late at night and guests were not allowed to play the piano in here anyway. Would he mind kindly stopping? The man did stop his piano playing and slowly stood up, tipping his hat politely to the manager before...*completely disappearing*. That was the manager's last evening on the job; he quit the very next morning.

Another more famous story is that of a woman who worked at the hotel. She was especially skeptical, and never told her husband or small son of the stories many guests would leave with her on their way out.

One day, on their way out to do some errands, the woman and her young son went by the hotel to pick up her pay (this being long before direct deposit was invented). As they waited in the lobby while the newer manager of the hotel went to get the woman her paycheck, her young son tugged at his mother's sleeve and said, "Mommy? Why is that man hanging there?" He pointed a pudgy forefinger up to the rafters, confused. The woman was also perplexed and did a little research herself, only to discover that the hotel she worked in had been a church prior, and indeed, one of the parishioners had hung himself from the rafters many years ago. That was all the woman needed to hear; she collected her last week of pay and quit the next day.

Today, employees won't go to the second floor; they refuse. They feel something is wrong up there, and once the history of the second floor, now used for storage, was uncovered, it's understandable. Cerviche's transformation from church to restaurant is well documented, but hidden in the now-trendy building is a bit of a shady past. The hotel slid a little bit, changing into a well-known brothel where plenty of well-known politicians and well-to-do businessmen would stop by and have their carnal fun. It was a business, one that many people looked away from as it thrived. Every once and a while, one of the prostitutes would find themselves in the awkward situation of being pregnant. Not wanting either exposure of their infidelity, nor another known heir to the family name, none of the politicians or higher-class men wanted the soon-to-be mother to actually have the child. It's uncertain whether they would tell their rich customers or try and keep it a secret, but once the prostitute gave birth upstairs, the known father would have the infant killed then and there.

Perhaps the most heart-breaking ending to this is what happens upstairs now. Visitors and staff alike claim to feel brushes and tugs at their shins and pant-legs and the sensation that something is playing with their feet, widely believed to be the spirit of the infants, crawling around on the floor as they never had a chance to do in life. It's a melancholy feeling, pressing down on people who enter, which is why many of the staff refuse to go up there.

Not every spirit who stakes its claim on Cerviche's is as tragic as this, however. There's quite a jokester with a penchant for female bartenders. This spirit, more like a playful poltergeist than anything else, will mess and play jokes with the female bartenders as they try and serve drinks. Once, a bartender, getting ready for the evening rush at Cerviche's, found herself with a burnt out light bulb near the bar. She grabbed a new one and placed it to the side while she took out the burned bulb. However, when she went to replace the socket with the fresh bulb, it was gone. For twenty minutes, she searched for the light bulb she knew she had set down on the table right next to her, but it was gone. Eventually, she found the bulb at closing time—nestled inside her purse in the employee's lounge.

The ghost likes to also throw things, mostly glasses from the bar. Sometimes the glasses smash, other times, they clang around and merely crack. Still, he is not a wholly unwelcome guest at Cerviche's. His presence is playful and a tad more mischievous than some would like, but nothing to raise alarms over. His presence is welcomed, and generally when he gets too out of hand, a cheerful reminder to please stop is all it takes to get him to back down.

Another sighting includes that of an African-American gentleman who likes to wave at passing, late-night partygoers. He's seen through windows and on the rafters of the restaurant, smiling and laughing a bit before entirely fading from sight.

With as many spirits in one restaurant as Cerviche's, one might think that was enough for a few mile radiuses, but not in the long run at all. This is only the beginning of Church Street Station's paranormal experience.

Bumby Block

Cattycorner from Cerviche's Restaurant is a building known as Hamburger Mary's Bar and Grill, but above the sign marking Mary's is another that says "Bumby Block." In 1885, it was once home to one of the finest hardware stores around, Bumby Hardware. Like much of Church Street Station, this store has gone through numerous transformations and remodeling. While the original wood from its earliest days remains the same, there's nothing to stir a spectral from the past into action like changing the building they reside in.

The little girl ghost seen in Bumby Block appears to be between six and nine years old, dressed in late 1800s period clothing. She is often reported having long, dark curly hair, and has a penchant for tapping on the windows and waving at passers-by. However, once attention is gained from a visitor, the little girl suddenly turns shy and...disappears.

Employees closing up shop at two or three o'clock in the morning have often witnessed a little girl skipping down the road. Obviously, a small child in a tourist district wandering out at such a late hour would capture anyone's attention, especially one skipping down the road. Running after her, calling for her to stop to see if she's lost, does little good in gaining any answers. She simply turns around, smiles at the well meaning do-gooder, waves, and disappears in front of them, a regular cheerful Little Girl Lost.

No one has any idea what her name is, or whose daughter she might have been. Joseph Bumby had nine children, including three girls; two of the girls were mentioned as grown and married, but I was unable to find out what happened to Ada Bumby. Did she meet a tragic end, or did she live a long and well life? Whoever the little girl is, she seems not to mind her afterlife, though she may not know she's gone from this life. No one has reported any negative feeling coming from what is now known as Hamburger Mary's Bar and Grill.

Bliss Nightclub

It's quite a different story for what is now known as Bliss, a nightclub down the entertainment block of Church Street. Even a person claiming to have the spiritual pick up of a stick could probably feel the violent emotions that run in the large coolers in the back rooms. There are two coolers used for storing supplies needed for a full night of dancing and partying at Bliss Nightclub; the first cooler, everything feels normal. It's just another refrigerator system. But it's the second one that employees will not go into at night, sometimes not even if they have to. Before opening for the evening, workers will go together and stock the bar; preparing everything they need in advance so no one has to go back to the second cooler at night.

It just feels wrong... the air is heavier there. Whatever made Bliss Nightclub suffer such a violent feeling, it's lingering. Not that Orlando was ever part of the old, Wild West; not many real cowboys have ever fought and died in what little bars Florida had in the late 1800s, but walking into that second cooler makes a person feel as though eyes are staring at them—and *staring* hard. Chairs and barstools are tossed around, but not in the non-threatening way at Cerviche's.

When renovations were first taking place, to turn the one-time restaurant into an actual nightclub, workers would first board the windows and continue working, installing new glass in the window frames. The plywood was boxed around the window frames once the glass was placed in, aimed to protect the glass from being broken from the outside in. But no one accounted for the glass being smashed by something on the inside. The last worker swore when he turned off the lights and locked the doors at closing time, the mostly-finished refurbished establishment was empty. But come time for the new workday to begin, the construction workers entered the main room to hear a strange tinkling sound. Looking everywhere for the source of the noise, they were astonished to find it coming periodically through the boxed around windows. Every piece of glass was shattered with the shards falling outside the now-bent frames. Something inside had blown the glass out, ruining the window frames, but no one could say what or who.

Bodies in the Furniture

Across the road from Bumby Block, now known as "Hamburger Mary's Bar and Grill," is an alleyway known as "Gertrude's Walk," which adjoins the railway system that is still functional to this day. It's easy to forget where the former avenue-turned-alleyway came from, but it was actually named after a former mayor C.D. Sweet's sister, Gertrude Sweet, in 1881. It's through this alleyway and to the right that the old funeral and furniture store owned by Elijah Hand used to be.

Elijah Hand bought the building from his business partner and took over the newly changed funeral business. Embalming had become more widely used during the Civil War, and in the 1880s, as Church Street Station was starting to emerge as a

Hand Funeral services used to be here, where it got so crowded, bodies would be placed on couches and chairs in the furniture store upstairs from the funeral home.

prominent part of city life, the new funeral home wanted to be as modern as possible.

But space was tight and money was needed, and with these thoughts in mind about using his property space wisely, Elijah Hand not only sold caskets, held funerals, and embalmed the dearly departed, he also sold furniture to the surviving family members. With his funeral business on the first floor, and his furniture store above on the second floor, Elijah discovered himself to have a fairly good head for business—until he started to run out of room to store the bodies of his cliental.

The embalming technique, still new in comparison to the older tradition of simply icing a body down to be buried the same day as the death, was wildly popular, and as his funeral business kept growing, Elijah Hand found himself running out of room in the morgue. The only solution he could come up with was to store the already embalmed bodies up in the second floor where the furniture store was held. When it was time for the funeral, he collected the appropriate body from the chair or sofa they were occupying and brought them down to the casket. Elijah switched around, preferring now to bring an asked for chair or table set down to the first floor, versus having a furniture customer travel upstairs.

Despite the somewhat elaborate set-up Elijah had in his building, he soon packed his bags when word got around that many of the new living room sets had had a dead body sitting in them before the living ones could bring them home. The building, like much of what is now in Church Street and downtown Orlando in general, underwent many changes until it finally settled as office buildings. No longer filled with embalming fluid or caskets, the building now housed cubicles and office desks.

In the 1980s, one such office moved in, using the second floor for its main offices. As I heard it, it was an insurance business, and fairly modern with its working moms. A lady who worked there brought her son in to play quietly in her office when she was short on babysitters. She didn't like this idea too much, and tried not to do it too often, but for a different reason than risking her boss' disapproval. The office, even while quiet, had its issues; often the woman and her co-workers found themselves witnessing things flying off of the desks, papers scattering everywhere. They would often come into work and find that chairs and desk knickknacks had been moved around without anybody understanding how or why things had been rearranged. It was alarming, but she, like everyone else, did their best to ignore it and not comment too much on the goings-on. But the more they ignored it, the more it happened.

It was getting increasingly difficult to find reliable babysitting, so she essentially had very little choice in the matter. Bringing her son to work, as he was far too young to watch himself, was

Many of the homeless have complained of the loud clattering of horses that go on throughout the night, even though there has not been a horse-drawn carriage down this road for many years.

Two orbs are visible, one on the far left and one on the far right. The far left one appears to be in motion. *Courtesy of Matt Thorne.*

the only option she had. Things were going well enough on the first day until the woman noticed her son was whispering and talking to himself, staring at the empty space in the corner of the office.

"Who are you talking to?" she asked, smiling and expecting the usually mundane answer of an imaginary friend.

"Mr. Roberts!" her son answered. "We're playing." And he pushed a truck to illustrate his answer.

"Oh? And who is Mr. Roberts?"

"He says he's the one who's always moving the stuff around, and making things fall. He says he's sorry if he scared anyone, but he just really wants you to know he's here," the son answered, and any thoughts of an imaginary friend were quickly gone.

But Mr. Roberts isn't the only spirit interacting with workers in the old funeral home. Every city I've come across has a Lady in White story to tell, and Orlando's is in Church Street Station, in the very same building. This Lady in White has kept her real name a secret, but apparently appears only to certain workers, dressed entirely in white, whispering in a low tone of voice to them. Some of the time, it's only snippets that don't seem to make sense, other times, it sounds so fast and hurried, there's no way to make out what she's saying.

The idea of such a haunted area is a little mind boggling, but there were reports of strange happenings from all the people at Church Street, including the homeless. Years ago, before a better community out-reach program was developed and used to help house many homeless people, the streets and bushes in front of businesses and buildings were the only place the vagrant could go. In the mornings, when businesses would open, a few very disgruntled would-be sleepers on the porches and bushes outside surprised the people. The homeless would complain and comment upon their loss of sleep because, as they said, the horses and carriages kept them up all night long.

No horse-drawn carriage or buggy or any type has been used in Orlando streets since the early 1900s, yet the clip-clopping sounds of horses pulling unseen carriages are heard, almost nightly going up and down the street.

Terror on Church Street

Orlando is, above all else, a traveler's maze. One major industry this city thrives on is tourism. It's one of the best ways businesses can think of to make tons of cash, and relatively quickly, because who isn't looking to have a great time on vacation? Theme parks, nightclubs, good dining—decorations and attractions must be bold, and edgy, something you can't get anywhere else. Universal Studios started offering an event in 1991 called "Fright Nights" around Halloween time, and later on, renamed for Halloween Horror Nights. The success was huge, a franchise that is still going on, and incited dealers and investors to try their gambit at creating a live, interactive horror attraction of their own, but not just once a year–all year long–in a twenty-three room building located off of South Orange Avenue, in the heart of Church Street Station.

Hi-tech special effects, ghouls, goblins, and wonderfully imaginative theater sets were built to provide frights and nightmares the whole year without any cartoonish quality. The scares, in fact, were so intense that after the attraction was set-up, children were not allowed to attend whatsoever. The only time children, relatives of a worker there, were in the building was during pre-production, and even that ended in tragedy.

During its construction, there was a fire in one of the theatrical sets in the building, which sadly claimed the life of two children, a boy and a girl, and a security guard. While the fire was not enough to close the building before it even opened, it did help instill the no children at all rule.

For eight years, Terror on Church Street was a huge success, but what was strange were the amount of complaints people would give to the managers at the end of each night—and they weren't about the attraction itself. It was always around the lines of, "I thought they didn't let children in here!" and "I can't believe someone brought their two kids in this place, it's way too scary."

A little girl and a little boy were often seen around various rooms of the attractions, as well as hiding and ducking behind the sets, and staring at the people walking through almost nightly, but when workers went to find any trace of the children, there was none to be found. No one had any idea where the children came from, or to whom they belonged, until someone mentioned the fire. *Real* ghosts in a haunted attraction, it would be almost ironic if not for the tragic origins of the ghosts.

One of the best pieces of evidence collected from Terror on Church Street is a tape from a security video camera. Usually, most videotapes are reviewed and if nothing abnormal is found, it's simply rewound and used again until the tape is worn out. But what was special about this tape was the misty specter it caught. Rising from the floor, the grayish mist seemed to slowly float up, right to the camera lens and, as it got closer, a man's face began to appear to the camera, closer and closer until the lens was obscured and nothing was seen but grey and then black. And then it simply vanished, leaving the room to appear as it had before.

Terror on Church Street is now closed, the reality company that owned the building sold it in 1999 after prices and a then-dying commerce took over. But the building still stands, waiting. No doubt, pictures taken in and around the building would produce some phenomenal orbs; *these three spirits want to be seen and acknowledged*.

Magnolia Avenue and Pine Street

Continuing down to Magnolia Avenue and Pine Street, Church Street is distinct in other manners, and that's in the ley lines surrounding this intersection. Interestingly enough, the streets paved out are a four way stop, and are surrounded by churches about half a mile from the Church Street Station area.

Ley lines, for those who may not be too familiar with this term, are alignments with places of ancient power, holy sites, and stone circles, to name a few. They are sources of power, drawn to places of worship, and spark with energy. It's not surprising that this area is supposed to be one of the most haunted areas in sheer volume. Spirits are drawn to energy; it's why batteries, fully charged the night before, will suddenly drain to nothing and electrical equipment will become disturbed. So it's not unthinkable that spirits would be drawn to stay in such a place.

On the corner of Pine Street sits the aptly named Pine Street Bar and Grill. It's a lively place with neon lights and several types of drinks; even the ghosts are in a partying mood. Several times, apparitions appear to be dancing to good, old-fashioned rock and roll. They're seen only from the upper legs and up, and will repeatedly go through the kitchen counters and dining room tables without disturbing a single piece of furniture. These good-time revelers never seem to tire, merely disappear after a while—*a residual haunt that never interacts with anyone.*

The other ghost, however, has no problem with interacting with people. Another prankster spirit on Church Street, this ghost seems to like to take glasses and push them to the other side of the bar. Many a bartender on the first floor of the pub have pushed a glass on the bar to pour a drink, only to have it suddenly appear somewhere else as they turn around for the bottle of alcohol they were looking for, pouring the drink right on the wooden counter where the glass *used* to be, in a comedy-cartoon sort of way. It's one of the few ghost stories I've been told that has made me laugh and say, 'Oh that's hilarious.'

Not as fun-loving or hilarious is the Clubhouse, another good-time party place in Church Street, right across from

Pine Street Bar and Grill. The tall, imposing green building is wooden, the original framework still sturdy and firm. The Clubhouse building is interesting because it's rumored to have been built on top of a Seminole Native American burial ground. It also happens to be in the center of the ley lines crossing Magnolia Avenue and Pine Street. The building itself is rumored to be ice-cold when a person walks through it, except for one spot in the back, where it's always hot and humid.

Drastic temperature changes aside, it's not so much the back room's inability to cool down that's startling, it's the view you can see late at night. The story I was told from one of the paranormal investigators who has set up research excursions in this building is that late at night, you can see figures that look to be, at first, like nuns in the classic black habits and robes. This confused him; he was sure there were no nuns in this area of Orlando, and couldn't name any convents in Florida at all. Most of the religious schools that still had nuns teaching wore regular clothing, and not the habits.

Still, there they were, walking around the building quietly without speaking to one another. The room felt hotter and more stifling than before. They disappeared for a while, walking, he assumed, around the rest of the building. Already guessing they were spectral images, the investigator simply wrote down his observations and he didn't figure he would see them again. However, he did, only this time, they were headless. Still walking in the same slow pace, the investigator didn't see them approaching this time...they were simply there as though they were in the middle of their nightly stroll, hands folded, their heads gone, leaving only stumps of necks visable to any person who happens to see them.

They were not nuns, as research later refuted; more than likely they were missionaries that met a messy and final demise. In never ending efforts to convert the Seminoles, the missionaries were sent to tribes and colonies, and sometimes when it became too invasive, the tribes decided the missionaries should be beheaded in the back and forth battles that ensued for many years, and it appears that not every remnant of this tumultuous time has been paved over and forgotten by cement and brick.

Directly across the street sits what used to be a restaurant, and now is an art gallery, at least on the first floor. But like many of the historical buildings down in the Church Street area, it used to be someone's home. The building is said to be haunted by a spirit reminiscent to a Mister Rogers.

This friendly male spirit is said to simply pace back and forth, up and down the second level of the gallery. During the day hours, he is respectably quiet as soft music plays and art collectors browse through the eclectic collections of oil paintings and sculptures. But closer to closing, the thumps and quick steps start up, and there are even reports of laughter, calm and kind. A sort of fatherly chuckle, if you will. With as many grisly ghosts as Church Street can boast, a friendlier spirit is a little refreshing. I imagined, as I heard the story of the gallery, with as many ghost stories and bloody tales floating about (no pun intended) the workers and owners of the gallery might consider themselves lucky.

On the opposite corner of Magnolia Avenue and Pine Street, the fourth and final building on this four way intersection is now closed. The two-story, dark green building houses many "For Rent" signs hanging in front of the dusty windows. What used to be there, years ago, was thought to be an aid for the community as a whole, a victim service building.

This was the place where people of all ages would call to get advice, or even just an ear to listen to them when they were feeling like they were in a rough place in life; advice on how to remain calm, someone who could help talk them out of hurting themselves or of hurting other people. Someone who could just listen and help wherever they could.

Of course, these were volunteers trained by professionals, but were not professionals themselves. Like all crisis call centers, they dealt with countless people, loads of callers, many times a day, a sort of stepping stone for people not getting professional help for whatever reason they may have. It was a place designed to help people, but not necessarily heal them, or make their situation suddenly and magically better. There were lines the volunteers knew they could not cross, and when to advise a caller to perhaps seek professional attention.

For as many calls as the workers at the victim service center received, they would still have their "regulars"—people who would call so often, many of the volunteers would know them by name and often phone number. One such regular caller is referred to as "Anna," who for obvious reasons remains nameless in any record that's left over from the victim service center due to confidentiality agreements.

Anna, would call, day after day, speaking to several volunteers, sometimes for hours at a time. To newer volunteers, she seemed stressed and like she needed a good ear to just sit and listen to her. To the more experienced volunteer, she began to become something of a nuisance. As calls wore on, she became combative and argumentative if the advice she was given wasn't to her liking. Presenting a problem to the caller, as though to guilt them to be on her side, the woman often seemed to feel the need to make herself out to be the helpless victim in all cases and problems. The world was against her, and while she was fighting valiantly, she needed someone to be on her side for a change.

Trained that idle coddling rarely helped anyone in a true crisis, but also knowing that they were not trained professionals qualified to give proactive advice, the volunteers were told to listen and give support, but not join in on Anna's verbal rampage. They knew they simply couldn't, and when the frequent caller began getting angry, demanding to know what they thought, the standard answer of "I'm here to listen and support, but I can't judge and tell you who's right and who's wrong," would simply enrage her further. Eventually, after scolding the volunteer who answered her phone call in the first place, Anna would huff and hang up on the bewildered volunteer.

Several times she threatened suicide if they didn't start taking her problems more seriously, and each threat was handled with care, trying to talk Anna out of doing anything rash. Numbers of free health clinics with doctors who could see Anna, with little to no charge, were offered, but to no avail. She kept calling, melting down, and getting angry when she felt she wasn't being helped.

After one such call, she cried, "You people never help me, why doesn't anybody listen to me?", and hung up. No one expected her to stay silent for long; they thought Anna needed time to cool off, and would call again in the next few days.

Anna didn't call again, at least not over the phone. That evening, she jumped off of her second story roof and died, committing suicide as she had threatened to many times before.

Perhaps she didn't mean to die; perhaps she thought she would break a bone and be sent to the hospital. Her actual death may have come as a surprise—an anger inducing surprise—because Anna is still in the old victim service building in Church Street.

So angry with not getting the help she thought she should have received, "Anna's" spirit is said to still be there, on the second floor where calls were monitored and taken. A common misconception about death and hauntings is that where a person dies is most often where their spirit will remain if they don't "move on" after death, but that isn't true. Often times, the spirit will remain in a place they felt most comfortable, or feel like being the most, sometimes out of love for the area, but sometimes still for spite and malice.

As far as malicious hauntings go, "Anna's" spirit is not happy, nor ready to accept help, just as she was in life. Determined to haunt the building and victim service center she feels failed her so badly, unsuccessful in preventing her suicide, the woman referred to as Anna is still there, despite the fact that the victim service call center is no longer operated out of that particular building.

Investigators walking around have reported getting off of the elevator, only to hear a whisper directly behind them, in their ear, saying, "Jump." It is a despondent place, with a feeling of resentment so fierce as to nearly be tangible. One investigator, Maria, who is a little more sensitive to paranormal activities than others, went to her knees, crying, and was unable to speak anything coherently until she left the building entirely.

I did not go into the building myself; the doors are locked and not open to the public anymore, the windows are empty, dark, and dusty. But as I walked with Joseph, my tour guide from Haunted Orlando, I could feel the hair on my arms and neck stand up straight, my skin prickling in goose bumps before Joseph ever opened his mouth to tell me some of the history on the building we were standing near. Even as he spoke the story in a matter of fact manner, I could nearly hear someone agreeing, "Yes, jump. This place never helped anyone. It's hopeless."

"Hopeless," as it turns out, is a good word to use in describing the way this building felt. Emotionally, it came across as the strongest building that I had been in or around, and I knew even if the invitation was open to explore the interior, I would not have gone in there. As if a physical barrier was between me and the doorway, I don't believe I could have crossed the threshold of the door. I don't claim to have a psychic bone in my body; any experience I've had with the metaphysical world, I chalk up to "them" contacting me for reasons unknown, and not because I have any special gift. But I maintain that some places, some buildings, have such an imprint left inside of them as to be oppressive, as to feel—for lack of a better word—just plain "bad." And much like Rouse Road Cemetery, the old victim service call center is an angry place to go in. I hope it's never re-opened or re-visited.

The Court House

Many buildings in Florida have been recycled for use; what's a daycare today may well be a bank in three or five years. The same rule goes for the more historic buildings, as was proven to me during my walk down Church Street Station. Buildings built and fashioned in the early 1920s still hold to their foundations, and in a crowded populated city like Orlando, any space that can work for a need is used, and happily so.

The former Orange County Courthouse was built in 1927, and for decades held the jail on the top floor; the living quarters for the jailer and his wife, an infirmary, and then separate cellblocks for men and women. Since the time it was actively used as a jailhouse, it has been transformed into one of the best and most innovative museums in Central Florida, known as the Orange

An orb captured right by Matt Thorne, left side (just out of range of his camera!).

My electromagnetic reader was going off like crazy around here, but nothing showed up in the picture.

County Regional History Center. Here, out-of-town visitors, local school children, and even residents can brush up on their local history; if they're lucky enough, they may run into a few spirits willing to give them their input on history as well.

I went inside the museum after-hours with the Haunted Orlando tour group. Joseph was my tour guide and he shared a few stories while the night guard unlocked the door for us. "The security cameras will catch a few things not explained," he said as we walked to the staircase that would take us up to Courtroom B. "The gift shop is closed up with that mesh wire door over there, but I remember one time after the last tour had left for the night, the camera caught a pair of sunglasses rise up and smash against the wire door without anyone being around. Couldn't explain it."

Floating sunglasses aside, the courthouse-turned-museum's real claim to fame is Courtroom B. It houses a table carved with the name of one of the most notorious serial killers America has

In the back of the room of the old courtroom, my reader went off again, but nothing visible showed up in this picture.

ever seen: Ted Bundy. Caught in Florida after a four-year killing spree, Ted Bundy was held for trial in different locations, one of which was the former Annex to the original 1927 courthouse. Witnesses say they saw him bent over the table during the entire trial, and it was later discovered that his name had been carved into the wood. While no one can prove it was, in fact, Ted Bundy who carved the name into the table, speculation heavily suggests it was.

Three spirits roam the old Courtroom B: one is speculated to be Ted Bundy, the other is a lawyer frequently seen pacing back and forth, and the last is a woman whose name is not known, but she stands in the back of the courtroom, very sad and despondent.

The room is kept shined to perfection; immaculate banisters and the solid oak entryway to the courtroom lend a heavy atmosphere to the museum.

When I visited the courtroom, I was glad I didn't go alone. Listening to Joseph give the history of the building and what went on in the courtroom, I wasn't entirely sure I would have been brave enough to venture around. Generously, he supplied equipment to use. One looked like a remote control with several lights on the top.

"What does this do?" I asked before we stepped inside. I kept craning my neck to see if I could catch a glimpse of the room. I don't know what I was expecting to see – *a disembodied head resembling Ted Bundy, or a floating woman in a white dress* – but the room was silent and empty, save for strings of white ribbon tied to several of the benches.

"This," he said, turning the remote on, "is an electromagnetic device. It lets us know when there's been a change in the atmosphere around us, an electronic change. It measures the charge in the air, and it's handy for telling us when something might be moving about that we can't see."

A picture in the Jury Box—I didn't feel particularly comfortable taking a picture in here.

A picture behind the defendant's table of the judge's bench. It's up here that the spirit of a lawyer has been seen pacing back and forth.

An electromagnetic reader used in the old courthouse now in the museum on Church Street. The lights on the left are green, and scale from green, to yellow, to orange, to red; red indicting a lot of activity in the area it's in.

I was allowed to sit in Ted Bundy's chair behind the defendant's table. Notice the orb in front and to the left?

In other terms, this remote was going to let us know if or when some activity occurred. Placing various purses and recording cases down, the four of us started to walk around the room. We all had our reasons for being there; me for my book, the newlywed couple on their honeymoon, and Joseph because this was his passion-turned-career.

"What are the white ribbons here for?"

"There was a wedding here earlier," Joseph answered with a straight face.

The newly married couple, Tabitha and Matt, laughed. Tabitha said, "People want to get married in this room? Do they know it's haunted?"

Apparently, they either do and that's the appeal, or they don't know and don't care to.

"Talk out loud, ask questions," Joseph encouraged us as he took a seat in the witness chair. The atmosphere was heavy in

The defendant's chair where Ted Bundy sat for part of his trial. His name is carved into the side of the table, and is now preserved by a plastic covering.

this room, and most of us were left tongue-tied. By this point in our walking tour, the four of us were fairly comfortable with each other, but none of us could think of a thing to say to any spirits that may be in the room. Finally, I asked a question, but to Joseph, rather than the spirits.

"So who's here?"

"There's three spirits in this room," Joseph said in a matter of fact tone, as though I asked him who the last three judges to serve were. "There is a lawyer who's been seen pacing back and forth, up and down the aisles in a worried manner, a judge, and one other spirit people think might be Ted Bundy."

Ted Bundy? Haunting here, of all places? However, Joseph cleared up the confusion. "A haunting may not be a person's specific soul or essence haunting one building, it could be just a piece of that person's essence or personality so deeply engrained in a place they felt a lot of emotion in." He pointed to a plastic covered area on the defense table where Ted Bundy's named had been scrawled and carved into the wood.

"He felt a lot of emotion here, being caught and arrested in this place."

We took a lot of pictures, and, interestingly, I noticed one swivel chair in the jury box kept turning to face us as we walked around the room. I did take a picture of it, and while there were several orbs caught in the pictures at the courthouse, funnily there was none by that chair.

I kept my electromagnetic reader out and on, letting the device guide me as a sort of downing rod, where I should take pictures. I got a lot of readings, not surprisingly, by the chair Ted Bundy sat at. It was then I noticed something odd with my camera.

"Hey. Weird, my battery is almost dead. It has a twelve-hour life, and I just charged it last night. It hasn't been used until now!"

Indeed, fifteen minutes before we walked into the museum that

The Jury Box in the old court room. One particular chair kept swinging to face the tour group. Notice the wedding decorations still up.

now holds the old county courthouse, I had checked my camera battery, and it was still full, not even showing the barest niche of draining.

Joseph laughed. "Yeah, he tends to do that. Always in that spot too. I learned a while ago to always carry extra batteries."

Still, I was a little disgruntled. '*Stupid ghost, draining my camera battery...*' was the first thing that crossed my mind. Out loud I said, "That's not cool. Leave my camera alone."

I didn't get an answer, but somehow I don't think that did any good.

The Jury Room

After the courtroom, our group left and gathered into the Jury Room, not too far from where we had been previously. The first thing every single person noticed was the temperature in this

Another faint orb, near the table, to the right.

This view of the Jury Room shows it as it is, looking normal. That didn't last long.

room. While the rest of the museum and subsequent courtroom was ice cold, a method to help both the displays and works of art stay preserved, this room was stiflingly humid, almost hot.

Spirits will mess with the temperature in a room, I remembered. Cold spots are simply more common than hot spots, but with air conditioning running all day and all night, the energy being gathered in would leave a frigid room more heated, not colder.

This was the jury room, where the juries would break and debate the case before them, but it was also once used as a playroom for children from the earliest days of the Orlando courthouse. When a custody hearing or trial that included the placement of a child or children came about, the children were kept in the jury room while the trial was going on. It was a sort of playroom, housing many years worth of children coming in and out of foster care.

Another orb by the light fixture. We really had a lot of activity that night.

Three spirits also are rumored to be here: a woman who stays in the back, a bailiff who used to work at the courthouse, and then little Emily. There is only very little information that's known about the adult female ghost. I asked about her, as it seemed an interesting place to haunt—a jury room that also doubled as a sort of childcare and nursery room? There is always a back-story involved, but sometimes, little concrete information to go on.

"What about the woman, why is she here?"

Joseph spread his hands apart. "Couldn't tell you. We brought in a psychic once, but the only thing she could tell us was that the woman was very, *very* sad and refused to move from this place. The only thing I probably can tell you with certainty is a lot of custody cases were heard here. Maybe it has something to that."

The largest orb showed itself in this picture.

A very faint orb was near Joseph, our guide from Haunted Orlando, located behind his back. Ironically, he kept feeling like he was being watched and then followed.

I agreed; there seemed to be a logical connection. If the woman had lost her children here and died later on in life, this area held meaning to her.

While there was no contact made with this woman, I felt we could all almost see her, back pressed up against the wall, clutching her thin hands to her chest, staring out at us mournfully. It was almost like a catch twenty-two to me: she needed help, but could not or would not make contact with anyone brought in. No one else could help her without her making contact. Or maybe she didn't want help to begin with. But still, I felt as though we were being watched, first from one corner, and then from another, always to the back of us.

The bailiff, as our group was told, stays fairly quiet, only glimpsed from time to time. He is never heard speaking or making his presence known other than to walk up and down

As Joseph changed positions, so did the orb moving to his right side, fading more.

the room's length, still guarding, and still on the lookout. I wondered if he was a residual haunt, not mingling with his surroundings or any changes, just doing the same things over and over again.

But by far, the most interaction that night was with Emily. Emily, we were told, was a little girl who had been placed in foster care in the early 1920s. She had been in the nursery playing while her case went on in the next room. But shortly after she was placed in foster care, she became very sick and died.

And here, it seems, was where she wanted most to be.

Joseph asked if we, as a group, minded if he turned off the lights and pulled out a teddy bear, a pig dressed as Easter bunny, and a small rubber ball. We said we didn't, and Joseph nodded. "Before I do turn off the lights, take a look under all the tables and tell me what you see."

We did, seeing nothing other than the bottom side of tables. Confused, I reported back there was nothing under any of the four tables or the stacks of chairs stored in the room. "Just tables and stacks of chairs," I said. "Used and worn down. Why? Are they supposed to be anything special?"

"Actually, no, and that's the point. I wanted everyone to see the tables are just tables. No tricks, no machines. Same thing with the chairs." Joseph walked around the room, laying the toys on the table as we got our electromagnetic readers and cameras ready. I understood why he wanted us to look; in order to verify any experiences we had that night, it had to be established that there were no tricks or fake "spooks" around.

The room itself was polished to a shine, and spacious enough to accommodate four adults walking around. The atmosphere felt a little more charged, but we were all much more comfortable than we had been in the actual courtroom. It was easier to talk out loud. Almost without speaking, our improvised "team" fell into silent places. Matt went to the corner of the room and started filming, while his wife, Tabitha, and I circled the area, chattering and asking questions. Joseph, ever the guide, was ready with his electromagnetic reader.

After a few moments, Tabitha and I stopped and looked at Joseph. He himself was also frozen, and held out his forearm for us to see. "I can feel...well, something," he said. I held my camera up and took several pictures of him. Later, when I reviewed the film taken there, a large orb revealed itself to be around Joseph in several frames...almost as if it were truly *following* him.

But at the time, I didn't have the chance to sit back and take a second look at any pictures I had taken. I just kept taking more, figuring I could look at them later. Out loud we asked questions, varying from "Do you want to let us know something?" to "Can you tell us your name?" With Matt recording, we weren't sure if

An orb of one of the spirits in the old Jury room right above Joseph's head.

we would get any EVPs or not and we were too caught up in the moment to think about a 'later.'

Gathered around one of the dented tables, Joseph produced the small rubber ball again. "Emily told one of our tour guides she wanted some of her own toys, so we got some for her." He gestured to the teddy bear, the Easter pig dressed as a rabbit, and the ball. "And these are Emily's toys, and just hers," he said aloud, speaking more to Emily than to us.

"Emily, you want to play ball?" Joseph asked and bounced the table hard on the table, as though to get her attention. We had fun with it the last time, didn't we?"

Apparently the answer was a 'yes' as Joseph placed the ball in the middle of the table. It wiggled once and then slowly started moving towards Joseph. It made a slow circle, backed up, and stopped in front of Joseph. He smiled, a sort of proud, indulgent smile. Tabitha and I stared at the rubber ball. We had both held it, bounced it on the wooden floors. It was a normal, everyday multi-colored ball, the kind you get in a gumball machine.

Those who believe in spirits would have educated us that Emily was simply doing what little girls do best: playing. But, while I believed in the unseen, I was still having trouble comprehending what I was seeing as Joseph slowly batted the ball away from him and we watched as it stopped, paused, and then rolled back to him.

"Hi, Emily," I said slowly, my eyes never leaving the rolling ball. "Mind if I play with you too?"

Joseph rolled the ball to me and I held a moment before rolling it back to the middle of the table, where it stopped, wriggled once, and then made a movement as though it was going to roll back to Joseph. For whatever reason, it stopped mid-roll and came back to me.

"She wants you to play," Joseph explained to me, and so I batted the ball back. It circled the very edge of the table for a moment before rolling back to me again.

It was a little awkward at first, but I soon felt at ease with this game of roll, stop, and roll again. "You know, Emily, I used to work at a daycare and nursery. The little ones there were younger than you, but we used to play games like this and sing songs all the time. Actually, I have a younger cousin who's about your age."

The activity around the ball increased, and soon, Tabitha was involved in our game as well. Funny enough, she had also been involved in children, as a former preschool teacher.

An idea caught me by surprise, but I went for it. Under normal circumstances, I would never have even entertained the thought, but I was interested in seeing if I could get Emily to work with me. "Emily, do you like to sing? Would you like to sing a song?" The nursery and daycare I worked for had been a religious school, full of Bible tunes and catchy songs with easy to remember lyrics. Luckily, Tabitha knew the songs as well. So, we sang to Emily.

Looking back on it, I cringe in embarrassment to think about the fact that in front of three strangers, I sang to a ghost child, but Tabitha did it too, and together she and I went through about six or seven songs, many of them gospel based, written for children. How many people can say they spent an hour playing with a little girl ghost, singing songs? The more we sang "Jesus loves the little children" and "The B-I-B-L-E, yes that's the book for me," the more Emily became active with the ball, and with more fervor. Eventually, Joseph simply took a step back and we watched the pig and teddy bear slide a few inches to the left and right.

The ball continued rolling, and when I picked up Emily's pig dressed as a bunny rabbit, and made it seem as though it were chasing the ball, the rubber ball itself bounced. Perhaps that was her version of a ghostly giggle? She clearly approved, and we played like this for a little while longer. The ball would roll, the stuffed animal in my hand would chase it, and the ball would bounce, roll, or tumble away in the nick of time, making the chase last.

The three of us made chitchat while Matt stood back and filmed. It was soon time to wrap up for the evening, and after we had said good-bye to Emily, Joseph put the toys and electromagnetic readers away; I went to gather my purse. I wiped some sweat off the top of my lip and was surprised when I looked down at my hand and saw the smallest traces of dried blood. Grabbing for a travel pack of tissues, I wiped my nose and upper lip; there wasn't a lot of blood, but I've never had a nosebleed before in my life, and it was enough to cause some alarm. When had my nose begun to bleed, and why? I didn't get a chance to ask before Joseph had turned the lights back on, so I tucked the tissue in my purse. Matt had stopped recording as well and I asked him, "Do you think she said anything to us? Something we couldn't hear?"

Joseph was the one who answered, "It wouldn't surprise me. Here," and went back to the case he had carried with him that held the electromagnetic readers. He unlocked it and pulled out a portable CD player, and held the earphones out to me. "She's spoken before; we're pretty sure it's Emily and not the woman who stays in this room too. Another investigator came with me when we recorded this EVP; she brought Emily the pig dressed as the rabbit for Easter a few weeks back."

I placed the earphones in my ears and waited as Joseph hit the play button. As the CD whirled and began, I could hear Joseph's voice with another woman I didn't know come through the speakers.

"Hi, Emily! Have you been a good girl?"

I could hear a knocking sound in the background, faint but there, before Joseph's voice came through.

"We brought some of your toys, your bear and that... pig-bunny-thing." I heard him laugh and the woman laughed too, a little chidingly.

"You like the pig-bunny I bought you, don't you, Emily?" she said and a small huffing-humming sound came through; it sounded like a small moan of agreement struggling to get through. It was as though the person was trying to speak, but couldn't quite get the words out. It sounded closer to the microphone than Joseph and the woman did.

"Right. Well, these are your toys Emily, all just for you. And no one can play with them unless you say, all right?" the woman continued, and she and Joseph broke off into a side conversation about the night's work. The soft huffing sound was heard again before a small voice overlapping the two speaking adults came on the recording. "Help me," the voice said, sighed, and then said again, "Help me."

Frowning, I stopped the CD and played it back a few more times. It was a short clip, only about thirty seconds or so, but I looked up at Joseph after I was finished.

"And you think this is Emily?" I asked him. I was confused; she had seemed playful, the very room which was unlike the rest of the museum, being hot and humid and stifling, didn't seem like a bleak place. Emily didn't seem sad to me. Not that I expected her to be thrilled about being departed from this life before she had a chance to grow up, but 'help me' sounded so desperate. Help her from what?

"Have you asked since hearing this what she meant? Help her from what, or who?"

"Yeah, the very next time we came out here, we asked several times, but she didn't say anything," Joseph replied as he snapped the case shut again. The frustrating part about paranormal investigation has got to be this: craving answers but getting none. The more you push for proof, the more you try to get an orb in a picture, or an EVP, the less you may find you actually get.

I didn't mention my bleeding nose. Maybe it was coincidence, or maybe I concentrated too hard on the energy flowing around the room. Or maybe it concentrated too hard on me. I can't say for sure it was because of the contact made with Emily that night, but if I were to give my honest opinion on explaining what happened to cause such a physical reaction, I would haphazard a guess that it *was* the communication with Emily that night.

We left the room, feeling the relief of the cold air on our sweaty faces and backs; the room's drastic temperature change was mind-boggling now that the four of us had left the jury room. "I have one more thing I want to show you," Joseph said as he ushered us into the elevator. We gathered around the back and let the door closed. Joseph stood by the control buttons, but simply let the door close behind him.

"Without pressing any of these buttons, the elevator will do two things. One, just sit here, and finally, it'll go down to the ground floor." We listened and nodded, wondering where he was going with this.

"At least, it's supposed to." Joseph smiled as the elevator did take us down one floor to the ground floor where the main entrance was located. But instead of stopping and opening the doors all the way, the elevators stopped mid-open and closed again, taking us up. Not to the second floor we were just on, but all the way up to the third floor.

"It'll do this all night, and only after closing hours when the building is locked up," Joseph waited as the elevator dinged, opened to show us the third floor, and then closed again, quickly.

Apparently, the museum has called the elevator manufacturer, for visits and inspections, but the strange floor selection after hours can't be explained. The elevators are on a hydraulic systems; no pulley ropes to become slack to end up on the wrong floor.

As the elevator doors opened for the final time that evening, I noticed Matt and Tabitha quickened their pace along with me. Joseph smiled at us all and said, "Congratulations, you've just had a paranormal experience."

I'm fairly sure we had been having them all evening.

Greenwood Cemetery

††††††††††

1603 Greenwood Street,
east of Mills Avenue and south of the East-West Expressway

††††††††††

Church Street has an interesting layout, ghosts and spirits aside. Part Old World charm placed in between skyscrapers and corporate offices, and daycares with playgrounds tucked behind wrought iron fences with trees planted around for shade. It's a little discombobulating to look to the right and see a cottage from the early 1920s, and then look to the left and see a municipal bank across the street. Even more so when you're informed that both buildings are in fact believed to be haunted.

Entrance to the acclaimed Greenwood Cemetery.

A calmer shot of Greenwood headstones and benches.

On my adventure into Church Street, I decided the best route would be to explore on my own before meeting my tour guide with Haunted Orlando Ghost Tours. It was early afternoon and after telling my supervisor I was off to go spirit searching, I was wished the best of luck and told my co-workers all hoped I made it back to work in one piece. It was a nice vote of confidence.

After overpaying for parking, I navigated my way to the main streets of Church Street Station. My goal was to locate Greenwood Cemetery, which was supposed to be near Church Street, and be back in time for my scheduled tour with Haunted Orlando around the area. Construction and half-finished renovations marred the way, making it more of a zigzag then a straight shot to the nearest building, a bank. My idea was to speak with some of the local workers, people more familiar with this area than I was.

It wasn't entirely easy to describe what I was looking for, or why I wanted to get to one of the largest cemeteries in

Orlando. Armed with a yellow legal pad and a digital camera, I probably came across as either one very strange tourist or a local quack. Still, I got the help I needed and was soon on my way. I decided to walk to Greenwood, thinking it was really only a few minutes away. As it turns out, the location of Greenwood Cemetery *was* only a few minutes away—if you're driving. Walking, it's about forty minutes away, if you jog at a quick pace. I kept hoping it would be worth the multiple blisters on my feet.

Even if spirits and paranormal activity isn't what you come to Greenwood for, the huge cemetery is pretty in a melancholy way. It's lacking the intense, nearly sinister atmosphere that the Rouse Road Cemetery has. Greenwood Cemetery was far more peaceful when I entered in the gates, and much larger.

The caretakers of Greenwood were helpful and thoughtful, as they provided a map for the public to navigate the sections, locating which plots were dedicated to what; family, war veterans,

It's a pretty expansive property.

hospital residents, and the multiple sections for babies and toddlers laid to rest.

I was excited to visit Greenwood, as I had heard that the Q section of the landscape was dedicated to the resting places of the Sunland Hospital residents, a place previously mentioned in this book. I felt like I had to see the result of "Sunnyland."

Were the residents truly at rest, or was there activity? As I walked the paved pathway (it's requested that the public not go into the headstone sections, but stay on the winding, paved driveway that loops throughout the cemetery as a matter of respect) looking for the 'Q' section, I wished suddenly that I had brought flowers for them. A paltry offering, to be sure, but I felt a little bit personal with those who lived and possibly suffered in a place I had written about. It would have been the closest I came to offering an apology on behalf of the living. It seems silly now, looking back on it, but what's felt in a cemetery doesn't often make sense after you leave.

Headstones as I tried to find the Q Section.

Greenwood Section Q — I finally found Section Q, the Sunland Residents' resting place.

The Q section was small; all of the graves were old and the print faded to near invisibility on the stone markers. How many were left there for good care by families, only to meet disappointing and early deaths?

The graves were sparse; compared to the other sections in the expanse cemetery, the Q portion was almost disappointing. Where were the other graves of the other patients and residents? I could only imagine that, hopefully, these sectors of graves were for people who didn't have a family to take them to a local resting place.

But I couldn't swear by it. A thought circled in my mind: *what happened to all the bodies*? Surely this wasn't it. So many residents died at Sunnyland, so where did they end up? As I've noted before, the most frustrating part of inspecting paranormal activity is the unanswered questions.

Sprinkled around Greenwood Cemetery are fascinating, though macabre, plots of graves called "Baby Land," numbered "Baby

Land 1," "Baby Land 2," and so forth, containing rows and rows of graves holding the remains of infants, toddlers, and very young children under the age of five.

On my initial walk around Greenwood Cemetery, I noticed brightly decorated fragments adorning the headstones and plots right away, even from the diameter edges of the grounds. But upon reading the small green rectangular signs that said nothing more than "Baby Land," I thought it was revolting and a tad ghoulish. "Baby Land" immediately brought to mind the photographs of the dead children, the kind from the late 1800s where they look like they're only asleep, but you well know they're dead.

It's probably the thought of any child, baby, or toddler dying somehow that's beyond sad. Activity surrounding the multiple Baby Lands is rampant, occurring both night and day around Greenwood. Tales of music, like a lullaby from a music box, tinkling out into the open air, are common enough, and sometimes even

Babyland 3, shortly before I heard the music and felt the tug on my purse.

Another shot of Babyland 3. People also claim to hear the voices of children, laughing.

the faintest wisp of laughter. Even though there aren't any music boxes around, people will still hear it.

Visitors have often claimed to feel a touch on their arms, or tugs on their clothing, even while alone. I hadn't heard any of these stories until after I visited Greenwood. After not getting much of an impression around the Sunland Residents burial ground, I wasn't sure if anything would happen at Greenwood at all. To be fair, I went around four o'clock in the afternoon, so I wasn't expecting anything phenomenal. It was still daylight out, and without the heavy atmosphere around, like what was at Rouse Road Cemetery, it wouldn't have surprised me if nothing extraordinary happened.

But it was around Baby 3, closest to the Q section, that, for whatever reason, I felt the need to say "hello" to out loud. There was no one else around me; the nearest person was merely a biker who was clear across the cement walkway.

"Hi there," I said aloud to no one. It was a hot, stifling day, with no breeze, but I distinctly heard the strong and sharp tinkling of a wind chime right after the words left my mouth. Surprised, I jerked my head around to see where it was coming from, but I didn't, or couldn't, see where. It was almost like an answer to me. There wasn't a breeze to be felt, and even if it was a wind too slight to feel, the metallic ringing sound went on for longer than I would have expected, starting and stopping again as though someone were playing with the chimes and then cupping a palm around the metal to stop the sound, and then starting all over again.

I stooped down on the grass; the Baby Land 3 plot was slightly raised on a small mound, displaying the headstones and memorial plaques better. Pictures, toys, and brightly colored knickknacks were everywhere, and if I had a mind to, I probably could have counted the angel statuettes by the handful.

"Hey, thanks," I said for no particular reason other than I felt the sounding chime was indeed a sort of answer. Was there someone thanking me for acknowledging them, or simply letting me know that someone or something was there?

Unlike Rouse Road, it felt lighter, completely different, softer somehow, more harmless. I wouldn't go so far as to say happy, but nothing gave any indication that this was a place of pain. Rather, it seemed to be a place of rest—as it was intended to be.

It was then that I felt a small tug on my left shoulder, where my purse hung. Looking around, I expected to see a squirrel at the very least, if not a person physically tugging on me. Was I not supposed to be kneeling on the grass? Of course, there was no one there, and by this point, I wasn't exactly surprised as I might have been before.

"It's almost closing time, I have to go to a few other places still. But, thank you," I said, half grateful that no one was there to hear me speaking aloud to a mound full of graves. But like I said before, you can't always predict what you may do in a cemetery.

It wasn't until I was on my way out the gates when I noticed my keychain was missing a figure on it, a trinket from Japan. One of my friends had ordered us matching figurines on a keychain to decorate cell phones or purses; mine had a cartoonish looking girl with green pigtails and a happy smile on her face. The tiny toy had dangled there for months, enchanting both my smaller cousins and many other younger children. It was colorful and looked like something fun to play with. But as I left the cemetery, I noticed only her head, which was strongly attached to the metal ring, remained. The rest of her body was gone. Immediately, I remembered the mysterious tug without a perpetrator while I was near the Baby Land 3 plot. Was that what happened? Had someone wanted my keychain, tugged, and ended up with only a body?

Bewildered and a little bit spooked, I hastened my pace. My next stop in the precious forty-five minutes I had before the gates would be closed and locked, was the veterans' plots.

Not surprisingly, the veterans' plots are also a myriad of activity. On the special occasions that the cemetery hosts moonlight walks

The veterans' section at Greenwood, where soldiers and shadows are seen amongst the headstones.

A beautifully calm area of Greenwood.

after closing hours, several shadows may stop and follow. At first, it seems confusing because people are walking and shadows are everywhere. But there will always be a few shadows *not* connected to an actual body—shadows that will move through the graves before disappearing behind a headstone or memorial, leaving the passerby to wonder what that was. After all, everyone else is staying on the appointed concrete walking paths, out of respect for the dead and the cemetery's rules. So then, who is making the shadow?

Asking around, one local man told me of the evening that he was out walking his dog on the paths that led up to the gate.

"I had just passed the lake over by the cemetery and I saw the figure of a man walking up and around the paths really slow. Just looking. He had a uniform on, like an old military uniform, and at first, I thought it was some sort of prank, since the gates were locked and closed.

"He looked solid, so I didn't really get what I was seeing at first. I just turned around and went home. It wasn't until later; I was telling my brother over the phone what I had seen, and how eerie it was to walk around the cemetery at night that I started to understand. Even my brother said, 'You idiot, you didn't see a real man, you saw a ghost.'"

Children laughing, music playing, shadows walking around are all a part of the melancholy Greenwood Cemetery. If you get a chance to go, I recommend it, even better if you can go during a moonlight walk or special event planned by the managers of the cemetery. Bring a camera and an open mind, and see what surprises you're able to find; just make sure your key chains are tucked away.

Orlando Downtown Theatre

One would think that by now cities would learn not to rip up graves to build large buildings on top of the sacred resting place of hundreds of people. Evidently, they have not.

Not far from Church Street Station, the land that the Orlando Downtown Theatre started out on was, indeed, a small cemetery or burial ground before it was ripped up and refurbished in the late 1920s. And, as with I-4, many experiences have happened since then...*ALL* pointing to a paranormal origin.

Before it was a theatre, the building laid out on the burial ground was actually a citrus packing plant, or so it started out. But immediately after the packing plant opened, there were a number of accidents: small fires, equipment failures, and more than once the roof had collapsed for no apparent reason.

Further investigation on the city of Orlando's part revealed the land in which the packing plant-turned-theatre was situated hosted a series of battles during the Seminole Wars and was actually used as a burial ground for the dead warriors.

Eventually, after so many failures and accidents, the packing plant was shut down and the building remained empty, until 1984 when it was reopened as the Tropical Theatre. Right away, the same accidents began to happen. Electronic equipment would fail; small fires would start from seemingly nowhere; plaster and plywood would rip from the walls, leaving large, gaping holes; the basement flooded, and eventually, rehearsals had to be done by candlelight.

It was only a matter of time before Tropical Theatre closed as well. Now the building is used merely for practice and acting workshops, but no actual productions. The same destructive accidents still occur, but on a smaller scale. While there has been no sighting of any physical manifestations of spirits, the coincidences remain unnatural. A building constructed on a burial ground having so many disparaging, almost violent, "accidents" can't simply be that unlucky.

Orlando's Naval Recruit Training Center

Also in close proximity to Church Street Station was the Orlando Naval Recruit Training Center. In 2002, it was torn down to make way for new landscaping projects. But just because the building is gone doesn't mean the stories of the second floor in Division Ten's barracks will ever be forgotten.

According to ex-recruits, they would do anything to avoid having to make rounds in Division Ten's barracks, especially on the second floor. And, especially at night. During the day, the second floor merely felt a tad creepy, but it was easier to brave it out for whatever task needed to be done up there. But at night... there was simply no getting around it. Someone would have to be the poor unlucky soul who had to walk around there at night and make rounds.

The entire floor would sound like it was breathing; a deep wet sound, rattling right into the recruit's ear. Despite that no one was stationed to live in the barracks on the second floor, the feeling that someone was indeed there and watching never went away. But the breathing sound was by far the worse, because the recruit would know he or she was the only person up on the second floor. At least, the only person left up there alive.

The bad feeling would follow the recruit like a mist; no matter where they went, the breathing would start up, and then quiet down, and then eventually start right back up again, raspy and ever present.

The building has since been torn down, but even though the cement walls no longer exist, it leaves one to wonder if the source of the raspy, thick phantom breathing still exists among the blank land.

14

Florida Folklore

I love Florida folklore, but mostly, I love the tales of ghosts and the frequent visits from Satan that Florida seems to get more often than not (gee, I wonder why?). The South is rich in its tall tales and folklore, and Florida is not deprived of that either, despite its transformation from sleepy Southern state to tourist and nightclub hotspot in certain locations. My grandmother told me many of these, or variations of. Some others were read about, and other still were told to me by word of mouth. Some of these folklores seem to have a ring of truth; the less outlandish sounding ones could very well be based on real events. But without any solid physical locations or dates to back them up, I can't, in all good conscious, claim them as true. Still, they make for some really nice entertaining reading. Without further ado, here's a collection of some of my favorite haunted Central Florida folk tales.

A Face in the Glass

Once, when Southern debutantes were more common to see and a larger part of society (even in Florida), there was a family who had a very beautiful daughter who was training to become a demure and perfectly mannered debutante. When it came time for one of the larger cotillions, closer to the debut of all the girls, there was a large tropical storm, bordering on hurricane status. Even though the daughter had planned for months to go to the dance, it was canceled, and the family decided to stay home and hope the turbulent weather did not take a turn for the worse.

Upstairs in her bedroom, the girl sulked and cried quite a bit, bitterly disappointed. She brushed her long hair while perched on her window seat and looked out the glass, glaring at the chaotic weather outside. Gales of water rushed at her window, thunder rolled, and lightning lit up the sky, but the girl was too angry to do much more than frown and pout at the glass.

Florida is known as the lightning capital of the United States for a reason, and sadly on this night, the girl was struck by lightning through the glass of her window and killed.

From that day on, there was an impression of the girl's head and hair in the glass of the window. Even when the family, still in mourning, replaced the glass and the window pane, the impression kept coming back. No matter how any times the family replaced the window's glass and painted the frame, the impression came back. After they moved away, the new owners came across the same problem. It's said that during debutante season and during any storm, no matter how small, the impression appears sharper than ever, the weeping of a dead girl can be heard through the walls.

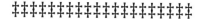

The Clock that Would not Keep Time

I always thought that a warning or threat cast over a town before a person was wrongfully put to death would be dire and deadly. Florida Folktales are full of them, but no one seems to listen to these condemned people. Of course, most times, the warnings and curses are more dire and dangerous than this...

Many years ago, a man was accused of a crime he had not committed. Throughout the whole trial, he professed his innocence and pled not guilty. But because he was of African descent, his pleas fell on virtually deaf ears, and though there was no evidence against him, he was convicted of the crime anyway.

Before he was sentenced to hang near the courthouse, the man said this, "Because I am innocent, but still you do this to me, your clock will never keep good time ever again." And with that, he was hung.

As the days and weeks went on, the townspeople saw that, indeed, their clock had stopped working altogether. Even when repaired, the clock would run fast, or it would run slow, its chimes coming out garbled and distorted. Every time the clock was looked at, the townspeople would cringe and shake their heads, reminded every day of their guilt by putting an innocent man to death. His prophecy had come true, because the clock never did run correctly again. And no matter how many times the clock was fixed or even fully replaced, the problem never changed.

The townspeople never forgot their crime.

A Christmas Gift

My grandmother, Patricia Branham, while she was born in New York, immersed herself in Southern ways of hospitality, cooking, and story-telling after she married my grandfather, Richard. I first heard this tale from her, but it has often been recollected and retold from diverse other sources and writers.

✝✝✝✝✝✝✝✝✝✝✝✝✝✝✝

An old Southern tradition says if someone comes up to you on Christmas Day, even if it's a stranger, and shouts "Christmas gift!" before you do, you are obligated to give him or her a present. This tradition is not very closely followed anymore – we have budgets, which apparently no one in the good ole days had – but keep in mind that there are no rules as to say what kind of present you need to give them! Insult the wrong person and it may be the last gift you ever want to receive.

However, more Southern folk back in the days of this tradition would consider themselves to be well mannered enough to give a thoughtful and respectable gift. As the tall tale goes, one Christmas Day, the Devil, knowing full well that God likes the balmier winter weather of Florida, hid himself behind a tree stump and waited. Sure enough, he didn't have to wait long before he saw God walking down the road; when the Lord came close enough, the Devil jumped out from the tree stump and said in a very quick voice, "Christmas gift!"

Now God, considering Himself to be both benevolent and well mannered, held up the end of the Southern custom, and said to the Devil, "Very well, you can go ahead and have the East Coast from June to November." Leaving behind a flabbergasted Devil, God continued on His morning walk.

So now the Devil can play with his hurricanes up and down the East Coast the whole summer and part of the autumn, which is why Florida has so many hurricanes. And because the Devil never keeps his word, he sometimes sneaks a few hurricanes over the western side of the Florida state, too. Merry Christmas, ya'll.

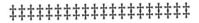

Orbs of White in the Cemetery

I can't really adequately describe how much I adore this story. It is, simply put, one of the funniest stories I've ever heard about a supposed haunting.

Back when Oviedo was more country farms than suburban homes, there were two sisters who lived together, alone. Neither had gotten married and seemed to like life just as it was. However, both sisters scared easily, and so when a few people in town started talking about large white orbs seen around the cemetery at night, the two sisters believed the story and quickened their pace whenever they had to walk by the cemetery fence.

One night, their trip back home from selling their eggs, vegetables, and homemade jams took longer than expected. It was twilight, with the sunlight dipping down low between the long and skinny trees. By the time they reached the gate of the cemetery, the two sisters had succeeded in scaring themselves silly, repeating the stories of how the white orbs would chase people throughout the cemetery, following them home, and sometimes even coming back to the house they followed the people to begin with. No one had gotten a good look at these white orbs or spirits, but truly, they must have been a fearful thing to behold.

From out of the elder sister's eye, she could see a large, white object, glowing all the brighter in the fading light. Taking the younger sister's hand, she gasped and pointed. "Do you see that?" she asked, and the younger sister trembled in fear.

"It's a spirit; it must be!" the younger sister squinted, trying to make out the shape. Suddenly, the orb moved, at a fairly fast pace; the only thing the sisters could see of it as it bobbed around the headstones was glimpses of white here and there. It was coming closer to them. Closer, and closer still, the two sisters could not move for fear, sure that they were going to be dragged into the underworld. Unable to face death with their eyes open, the sisters clung to each other and closed their eyes shut.

A moment passed. Then two, then three, and finally, the elder sister cracked her eye open just the tiniest bit. Standing in front of the two sisters was nothing more than an old goat chewing on some ivy leaves that grew around the cemetery gates.

The two sisters hurried home and did not mention the incident to anyone for many years.

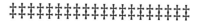

Why Florida Moss Hangs on Trees

Over the years, I've heard various tales of how Spanish moss came to be, from a bride's chopped off braid coming to life to escape her abusive husband, to an old man's beard hopping from tree to tree in an attempt to see the world, but this one – the legend of the woman's hair following the soldiers – is by far my favorite version.

Why they would have told this story to a group of wide-eyed second graders, I'll never know.

One of the first Florida folklore I heard involving ghosts was on a field trip to Fort Christmas, a park and historical museum off of Highway 50. There they gathered a bunch of squirming eight-year-olds, promising an hour at the playground afterwards if we sat still, and for goodness' sake, behaved.

Our trip featured explorations of the various forts turned into museums of everyday life at the once-working pioneer military fort. Our storyteller was an older gentleman, someone who our teachers told us, was a Creek Indian tribe member, or what we now called Seminole Native American, and who looked a lot like our various older, kindly uncles. I don't know, to this day, if he really was a Seminole Native American, or if this was just a story someone made up. But on this particular field trip, he sat in a chair while the rest of us gathered at his feet on a bed of prickly pine needles, staring up at him. The humidity clung to our shoulders and our hair, but the older man, who told us to call him Mr. Jim, didn't seem to mind.

He began the folklore session by telling a few jokes to make us laugh, and launched into stories of the wilderness in the 1830s and 40s, as though he lived through them himself. Mr. Jim was an older man, so for all our child-minds knew, he probably had.

At the end of the hour, he leaned in to us and spoke in a lower toned voice than he had. "Do you children know why Spanish moss hangs on the trees like that?" He pointed a blunt, leather-like finger up to the canopy of trees. We didn't, but, fairly sure it was a scientific answer, we waited, prepared to be bored again.

"In the old days, my people moved from their original homes, and came here. Our names changed, but not our pride, not our people. We came here, and other tribes from nearby joined, making us stronger than we had been before.

"But in those days, there was war and battle. Soldiers came and went, and we tried to live as best as we knew how. For years, they tried to make the tribes leave Florida, but we wouldn't, so we fought. For seven years, we fought each other, aged war. There's a legend that one day, a woman was captured by a soldier.

"She was held as a captive, and the captain decided he'd cut off her head and put it on a pike outside the camp as a warning for anyone who dared to defy him. The woman was brave and did not plead for her life. But she looked and spoke to him, very seriously. 'If you do this horrible act,' she said, 'it will follow you where ever you go.'

"The captain laughed, because she was only one woman; what could she do? How could she possibly hurt him if she were to die? So, ignoring the woman's warning, the captain did just that, killing her and cutting off her head, putting it on a pike outside of his tent. Now this woman had very long, very black hair that spiraled down her back...when the soldiers sawed her head and placed it on the pike, the black hair went grey almost instantly. The other soldiers were scared to see this transformation and began to take the woman's curse seriously, but the captain still did not believe. 'She is only one woman,' he told his troops. 'What can she do, dead and gone?'

"But not so. That night, the captain woke up in his tent to find the bodiless head turned on its pike, staring straight at him, her now-grey hair swaying in the breeze. The woman had died with her eyes open and nothing they did could make them close again. Panicked, the captain moved the head on the pike further from his tent. But in a couple of hours, he awoke again to see the pike back in its original place by the opening of his tent, staring at him. Again, he moved the head, but again he woke to find it there, staring at him through the grey hair. Unsure of what else to do, the captain ordered the men to take the head and bury it somewhere off the campsite. The soldiers did what he said, but they still remembered her words: 'If you do this horrible act, it will follow you where ever you go.'

"The captain tried to calm himself, repeating over and over that the woman was dead, that she could do nothing to hurt himself or his men. The next morning, the head had not returned, and the captain considered himself a smart man indeed for thinking of a good way of getting rid of the head. Perhaps one of his soldiers was playing a trick on him.

"But after the sun rose, one of the other soldiers pointed up to the large trees. 'What's that?' he asked, and the captain looked up. On the lower branch, a clump of tangled looking, dark grey moss hung down, thick and curling around the branch. It looked like the woman's hair. Snatching the moss, the captain threw it to the ground and told his soldier it was nothing, nothing at all.

"Deciding he had had enough, the foolish captain told his troop to break camp; they were going back to the base, miles and miles away. He knew the woman's tribe would be waking up to find her missing, and would come soon for revenge. Thinking his escape was the best possible plan of action, the captain and his soldiers packed up and left.

"Soon the traveling group of soldiers noticed that wherever they stopped, they saw more of the strange grey, tangled hair hanging from the trees, as if it were following them. Everyone thought of the woman's words: 'If you do this horrible act, it will follow you where ever you go.' But not wanting to risk the wrath of their captain, the other soldiers said nothing and tried to ignore it. Soon, they had traveled many miles, and into many other states up the eastern coast to South Carolina.

"By now, the grey moss was everywhere, on nearly every oak and cypress tree the soldiers could find. It was thick, and on the higher limbs so they could not even pull it down. Scared out of their wits, the soldiers did not know what to do. Every tree had the woman's long grey hair hanging from it, watching them. As the wind blew, the captain began hearing the woman's voice through the moss, whispering her promise. Every twig that snapped, every noise the woods made around them made him jump, sure that the woman would come back to get her revenge.

"By the next morning, the soldiers woke up to make the last leg of their journey. When they went to wake the captain up, he was not in his tent. They searched until they came to a large, crooked looking oak tree. There, hanging by some spare rope, was the captain. The grey moss had already grown around the rope, hanging by the captain's head. Horrified and convinced they were all cursed, the soldiers quickly cut their captain down and hurried the last few miles back to their base. Never until they were old and dying did the soldiers speak of the woman and her grey hair, but just as the woman promised, she followed each one, wherever they went. You'll find her moss-hair in Hawaii, South Carolina, and even other countries. Wherever the soldiers scattered to, the moss followed. And those men never forgot the woman's words, because she had made true on her promise."

Mister Jim took a breath and leaned on his knees towards us. "Most everyone knows this moss by the name of Florida moss, because it originated here. Or so the legend goes."

†††††††††††††††

Yet another variation of the Spanish moss tale involves a slightly clumsy Spanish sailor with unfortunate luck in the ways of courting and love.

After yet another failed attempt, he decided to venture to the New World on ship and leave his troubles behind. If he could not have love, he would have riches and woo the ladies that way. Upon landing on the coast of Florida, the entire crew set out and set up camp right in the middle of the state.

It was there he found some of the most beautiful Indian maidens he had ever seen, bathing by one of the larger lakes. Their skin was golden brown, and their hair was so black it looked blue. Overcome by the wonderful sight, the Spanish sailor decided to chase one of the maidens around the lake.

Laughing at such attention, the Indian maiden decided she rather liked this new game and scurried off into the wooded area, where they would not be so easily seen by disapproving eyes. Delighted that his luck seemed to changing, the clumsy sailor charged ahead, and followed. Even when the maiden slipped up the tree, the smitten sailor followed, despite the fact that his footing was not sure.

When he finally reached up to get her, the sailor lost his balance and fell, catching his head in between two sturdy branches. Screaming, the maiden fled from the tree, and while the sailor's body decayed, his beard grew and grew, eventually jumping from branch to branch in search of his beautiful maiden.

‡‡‡‡‡‡‡‡‡‡‡‡‡‡‡‡‡‡‡‡

Room for One More

I've heard so many variations of this story, it didn't surprise me to read Florida's version; combined with stories from co-workers, friends, and family members, all interjecting with "Well, I heard it this way..." Many people have heard this folktale, as just about every state has its own version. What makes this version differ from the others people have read? Probably not much, the details stay consistent throughout the multiple versions. It seems Death has traveled around the United States many times.

†††††††††††††††

A girl from Atlanta, Georgia decided to move down to Florida for college. Having grown up in the smaller county of Atlanta, she was unsure of what to expect from a new home and ended up right smack in the middle of the Sunshine State.

On her first week in town, the girl and her parents went exploring around her new college campus. It was larger than expected, many of the classroom buildings having elevators to take students and faculty to the third or even fourth floors.

The girl waited behind the rest of the new incoming students, all touring with their parents as well, when behind her, the elevators opened up. Standing there, an older man with long white hair and a grizzled beard grinned and crooked his fingers at her. "There's room for one more," he said in a deep voice and cackled. Disturbed, the girl gave a startled scream, but when she told her parents, they did not believe her.

The girl knew she had seen someone, and decided to avoid the elevators on campus if she could. The next week, the girl met with a few of her classmates at the library to work on some upcoming projects. Her peers suggested the fourth floor to study, as it was quieter. But when the elevator opened, the girl saw the same man with the white hair and grizzled beard. "There's room for one more," he croaked out again. The girl screamed again and pointed, certain that her friends had surely seen what was right behind them. Unfortunately, not one of them claimed to see the old man.

By this time, the girl avoided all elevators entirely, trudging four, sometimes five flights of stairs to get to her classes. The humidity made the heat seem to cling to her skin, made her sweat, and going up and down stairs all day did not help, but still the girl was adamant about what she saw in the elevators.

Final exams came near the end of the semester, and suddenly students who had not shown up much for class during the weeks prior were in a frenzy, studying and trying to make their grades up. In one of the large buildings, the elevators were full of students, going up to the fourth floor labs. At the risk of being late to her final, the girl started to reconsider taking the stairs all the way up. But when the elevator doors reopened to let more students in, sure enough, there was the white-haired old man, his eyes bugged out; he laughed and crooked a finger at the girl. "There's room for one more," he croaked.

The girl once again screamed and backed away, fleeing the building. It was only later, when the fire trucks and ambulances crowded the campus that the girl learned how the elevators had free fallen once they reached the fourth floor. With so many people overcrowding the elevator, a few people were badly injured, and several more were dead.

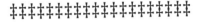

Pumping Water

Though Lafayette County is a bit farther than Central Florida, this folktale was too good to pass up. I've heard several variations to this tale, and I've also heard it called "The Wife Who Wouldn't Wear Pants," about a wife who would never wear pants while entertaining company. I'm not sure if the implication is she'd walk around in a skirt, or with nothing on besides her shirt.

Much of the farmland in Florida has been turned into suburban housing by now, but some remains of a "simpler time" are still around. In Lafayette County, there's a plot where an old farmhouse used to be. The farmhouse itself is gone, but an old water pump is there. On nights when the moon is brightest, the shape of a woman can be seen working at the water pump.

The legend says her husband chopped her head right off her shoulders in a fit of jealousy over his wife's socializing ways. He was a farmer, born and raised in Florida by other hard-working farmers. Through some bout of luck, he managed to marry a "city girl," who, while no help around the farm, was pretty and charming, and could usually smile and flirt her way out of trouble.

He would come home from working in the fields, or selling his orchard crop, or livestock, sweaty from the fields, and there his wife would be, swishing her skirts, and entertaining some people he didn't really know. Other farmwives helped around the house; cooked good meals with simple foods, cleaned, worked with the animals, but not his wife. She would not even do the simplest of chores, like bringing in fresh water; she was too busy having an enjoyable time with strangers in his house, some of them men.

The husband stewed over this for many months, rumbling quietly to himself whenever his pretty young wife asked him what was the matter. She would, more than likely, get back to whatever she was doing without waiting for an answer.

Eventually, after such a gathering in his house, the husband stormed over to his wife, grabbing her by the back of the neck. "Who was that man you had your eyes all over?" he growled.

"No one, he's just a friend from in town! He works at the bakery," his wife gasped out, fear starting to gnaw at her.

"You're always with someone, you never help out around here! Get out that door, you're going to do something useful if it's the last thing you do," he shouted and with a powerful shove, pushed his wife out the front door, watching her stumble down the porch steps in her heels and party dress.

The rage the usually placid farmer felt now bubbled inside his gut, to his chest, as he watched his wife walk where he pushed her to, to the water pump. She started to cry over her ruined shoes, the rough way he was treating her, and proclaiming her innocence. "I haven't done anything wrong!" she wailed when they reached the pump. "Why won't you believe me?"

"Pump the water, do it now!" he husband spat out, throwing a bucket at her feet.

"No, answer me! Why won't—" But the wife never got to finish her plea. Enraged by that simple 'No', the husband reared back and took his axe from where it lay on the ground, swung it in an arch, and lodged it in the side of his wife's neck. It took two more blows to sever her head from her neck.

Blood pumping in his veins, the husband's ragged breathing was the only sound the farm heard for a long time. His wife's body slumped over on top of the water pump, her pretty young head sitting a few feet away. As he calmed down, the husband gaped at the sight before him; what he had done? What had he done!

Taking his wife's head and the axe with him, the husband trudged back into the house, numbed, and quickly tied the bed sheets together to make a noose. He hung himself in the house, and it was not until the next day that their bodies were found when some of the friends of the wife drove down to see her for their usual get-together.

It was not long after that the farmhouse and barn mysteriously burned down into ashes, and the only thing left standing was the water pump. Now, on nights when the moon is the brightest, the pump can sometimes be seen pumping water out by itself, slowly, as though someone not used to working the handle is trying to get water. On other nights, the shape of a headless woman is seen actually pumping the water with slow, jerky movements, moaning quietly for her head.

‡‡‡‡‡‡‡‡‡‡‡‡‡‡‡‡‡‡‡‡‡

Florida's Own Headless Horseman

I know. I was surprised too! Florida has its own headless horseman tale? I feel a bit proud. Of course, after reading this folklore, I was able to easily see why the poor soldier became headless....

Twenty miles before you get to Kissimmee, but still in Central Florida, there is a large oak tree, hundreds of years old. It's known to Florida natives as Deadman's Oak, and for an understandable reason.

When it happened, not many know, but it was long ago, as legend has it. A young pioneer, eager to prove his worth, was coming up on the trail between Lake Kissimmee and Lake Gentry. On this trail, a large creek cut through the then-wooded area, however a sturdy bridge had been built in order to give safe passage. Beyond the bridge stood the oak tree, only slightly smaller than it is today.

Some people say he was delivering a message to the other pioneers fighting against the enemy Spaniards, and others say he was merely riding home. But the young pioneer, perhaps too eager to relay his message or see his loved ones again, made the mistake of choosing to ride a white horse (although some say it was the only horse left for him to ride). To get to his destination, the other side of the bridge and just beyond, the young pioneer had to travel through enemy territory.

But he was traveling at night, making the white horse appear all the brighter. It was then that Spaniards ambushed the poor man; he was captured and beheaded only miles away from his destination, thus giving the then-nameless oak tree its title.

Every night since that time, at midnight exactly, he comes back, riding his white horse and looking for his head. Unlike his ghoulish Washington Irvine counter-part, this headless horseman does not chase any unsuspecting Ichabod-prototypes. He seems to ignore people as he rides his horse around Deadman's Oak, simply looking for his head.

Ghost Baby aka The Wail at Dark-Thirty

Growing up, my chief source of income before my first "real" job was babysitting. I'm glad I never heard this folktale back then, or I would have been a very broke teenager.

Surprisingly, ghost baby stories abound in many cultures, originating in Latin American countries, so it's not unexpected to hear some from a Floridian perspective. The term 'dark-thirty' is a term used in the southern states to mark the time of day as the sun is going down, and it's usually when the spirits start to roam and call out. I wonder what would happen if we answered them?

✝✝✝✝✝✝✝✝✝✝✝✝✝✝

The twilight hour in the South is the time the spirits will call out to you. So don't be fooled; the keening sound you hear that you dismiss as the wind might not be...it might actually be a ghost baby.

Several accounts claim the cry of a ghost baby could be chalked up to the howl of a lonesome animal, or the wind whistling through the palm trees. But if you dare to venture out to find the source of the cry, be very careful...because you might actually find it.

The place you'll find it will not be a very good place to find anything, really. Because what you will find making the noise will be a baby, and the place you will find him in will be a clearing in the middle of the woods.

Swaddled and looking as sweet as can be, the crying will stop as soon as you get close to the baby. He will be laying near a tree stump, usually a jagged-looking one that's leaning over. When you pick it up, the poor thing will smile its dimpled cheeks at you and weigh very little. You may even coo and smile back at it, and think, *how can anybody leave this defenseless little baby out like this?* Snakes slither rampant in Florida summers; hurricanes do too. Thinking about what could have happened to the infant makes you shudder.

Of course, you have to take him home now and call the police. Someone abandoned a baby in the middle of a clearing, in the woods! It's the right thing to do, to take the little thing home.

But when you hold the baby close and start to leave the spot, the baby will stop cooing. In fact, he will stop making noise all together. If you look down, what you might see are a pair of frank blue eyes staring back at you, in a way no baby should. But otherwise, he looks the same as when you found him.

If you decide to keep walking back to your house (or back to your car, however you got to the wooded area), you'll notice something else that's funny. The baby seems to be a little heavier. And with every step you take, he gets heavier and heavier until you will notice your arms starting to ache. And then, you will look down at the baby.

And find the baby is not a baby anymore. The body is still small and wrapped up, but the face is that of an old man's, wrinkled with tufts of grey hair. The old-man baby will smile at you then, showing a row of sharp fangs behind withered lips. Of course you will be startled, maybe even scream. Don't worry, I would too. You might even drop the baby (don't worry about that, either, I'd do the same). But instead of the baby actually hitting the ground, you will hear nothing. The baby with the fangs and old man face is simply gone. But from the spot you found him in, the wailing cry you first heard begins again. Only this time, I'm not very sure you would go back in again.

A few variations apply to this story in particular. Some say that Florida swamps and wetlands are where you'll find the ghost baby; others say it's always in the graveyard, and the baby appears on his grave, angry that he never had a chance to grow up. Other tales have the baby found in the middle of the woods, like this one, near dead or dying tree stumps.

Some others believe the ghost baby's face just turns into an old man and gets heavier, and that he must be returned to the grave in which he was found. Still others maintain that the baby grows larger and eventually turns into a demon with horns and a tail and sharp claws. Either way, it was fun to play around with this Florida folktale, but I am not, by any means, the first one to come up with it!

‡‡‡‡‡‡‡‡‡‡‡‡‡‡‡‡‡‡‡‡‡

Yankee Blood on the Floorboards

Once again, as with many of the folktales I've heard and read, this one may actually be true, but because I can't pinpoint an exact location for it, or names and dates, it'll have to remain at "folktale" status for now. Still, if you find yourself in an old house in Winter Haven, check the wooden floors for any odd stains.

††††††††††††††††

Florida, while not as deeply ingrained in the Civil War as most states, saw its share of battles, some of the better-known battles taking place in Narcoosee. However, Winter Haven in Central Florida was the scene of several battles, many of them spilling over into residential areas of both the towns and rural farmland.

Often, both battalions would seek shelter in the actual homes, with family members still left inside, sometimes by invitation, and other times by force. One such example occurred with a Union soldier, making his way into a Confederate household (that's to say, a Yankee asking for a meal at a Southerner's house—not the best and brightest idea). However, after battle, a Union soldier did come across a farmhouse and demanded to be let in to rest and get something to eat. Separated from his unit, the soldier knew he would die traveling on his own; surely he would be shot or captured if he continued traveling for the night.

The woman who lived there had her son and husband fighting for the Confederate side, and staunchly refused to let the Union soldier in. The Union soldier grew angry and shouted, "If you don't, I'll break down the door and shoot everyone in there," he yelled. Fearing for herself and her two young children, the woman allowed the Union soldier to push pass her, spitting on the ground after he did so.

Grounding her hate and fear deep down inside, the woman suddenly became very hospitable towards the soldier, offering him a place at her table and food to eat. The soldier, weary from battle, ate his fill, and lulled by the heavy food and drink, started to doze at the woman's table. The woman, believing this was her only chance (for surely the soldier would kill her and her family anyway, or so she thought) ushered her two small children to bed and told them not to come out no matter what they heard.

After the children tiptoed out, the woman picked up the axe used for chopping firewood that was left by the stove, and without a moment to lose, struck the Union soldier's head. Blood gushed to the floor as the soldier gasped and sputtered until he was dead, twitching where he still sat, slumped over the table.

The blood ran on the ground, staining the wood floor by the fireplace. No amount of scrubbing ever cleaned the floor by the stove—the house still stands today with the old bloodstain still on the floor, deeply embedded.

I've heard a slightly twisted ending to this tale as well. On quiet nights, muffled thumping sounds can be heard that sound like a body being hit with a thick, sharp object, and falling. Then, silence. It's on the nights that the thumping noise is heard that shortly after comes the scent of fresh blood, almost overpowering in the room. Having never been there myself, I can't say for certain it's true, but the violence waged in that house certainly makes it a perfect candidate for an old fashioned haunting.

Resources

- Reaver, J. Russell. *Florida Folktales*. Gainesville, Florida: University Presses of Florida, 1987.

- Many sources used were via interview. Many heartfelt thanks go out, especially to Emilio San Martin of Haunted Orlando Tours, Mary Lee Gladding-Swann, Elizabeth Liebel, Matt and Tabitha Thorne, and everyone who wanted to remain anonymous but still took the time out to speak with me.

- Photographs of the Dead Zone on Interstate 4 were used with permission by Mike Holfeld, investigative reporter for WKMG TV, Channel 6 news. Pictures of St. Joseph's Colony and historical artifacts were generously donated by the Orlando Museum.